Fix-It and Forget-It®

FRESH & FLAVORFUL

Fix-It and Forget-It®

FRESH & FLAVORFUL

No-Fuss Meals for Your Slow-Cooker or Instant Pot

HOPE COMERFORD
Photos by Bonnie Matthews

New York, New York

Photos by Bonnie Matthews

Good Books books may be purchased in bulk at special discounts for sales promotion, corporate gifts, fund-raising, or educational purposes. Special editions can also be created to specifications. For details, contact the Special Sales Department, Good Books, 307 West 36th Street, 11th Floor, New York, NY 10018 or info@skyhorsepublishing.com.

Good Books is an imprint of Skyhorse Publishing, Inc.®, a Delaware corporation.

Visit our website at www.goodbooks.com.

10 9 8 7 6 5 4 3 2 1

Library of Congress Cataloging-in-Publication Data is available on file.

Cover design by Kai Texel
Cover photo by Bonnie Matthews

Print ISBN: 978-1-964219-06-6
Ebook ISBN: 978-1-964219-27-1

Printed in China

Contents

Welcome to *Fix-It and Forget-It Fresh & Flavorful* 1
Choosing a Slow Cooker 1
Get to Know Your Slow Cooker . . . 5
Slow-Cooker Tips and Tricks and Other Things You May Not Know 6
What Is an Instant Pot? 9
Getting Started with Your Instant Pot 10
Instant Pot Tips and Tricks and Other Things You May Not Know 12
Instant Pot Accessories 14

Recipes

Breakfasts 15
Soups & Stews 37
Chicken & Turkey 39
Pork 55
Beef & Lamb 63
Meatless 69
Main Dishes 83
Chicken & Turkey 85
Pork 109
Beef 121
Meatless 147
Seafood 159

Side Dishes 167
Desserts 199
Metric Equivalent Measurements 214
Recipe & Ingredient Index 215
About the Author 225

Welcome to Fix-It and Forget-It Fresh & Flavorful!

Want to spend less time in the kitchen without sacrificing the freshness and flavor of your food? If your answer is a resounding "Yes!" then this is just the book for you! Within these pages, you will find 127 recipes for your slow cooker, Instant Pot, and even a few adaptations for your air fryer, to help you find the freshness and flavor you're looking for. You won't need to spend a crazy amount of time in the grocery store hunting for strange ingredients or hours prepping ingredients. We've tried to make these recipes as easy as possible, with clear, concise directions, allowing you to put food fresh food on the table in the quickest amount of time possible.

Bring your kitchen to life with recipes like Spinach and Mushroom Frittata, Creamy Butternut Squash Soup, Pasta Primavera, Hungarian Beef with Paprika, Chili-Lime Corn on the Cob, and Upside-Down Apple Pie. There is something for everyone in this cookbook. We hope you enjoy these Fresh & Flavorful recipes time and time again!

Choosing a Slow Cooker

Not all slow cookers are created equal . . . or work equally as well for everyone!

Those of us who use slow cookers frequently know we have our own preferences when it comes to which slow cooker we choose to use. For instance, I love my programmable slow cooker, but there are many programmable slow cookers I've tried that I've strongly disliked. Why? Because some go by increments of 15 or 30 minutes and some go by 4, 6, 8, or 10 hours. I dislike those restrictions, but I have family and friends who don't mind them at all! I am also pretty brand loyal when it comes to my manual slow cookers because I've had great success with those and have had unsuccessful moments with slow cookers of other brands. So, which slow cooker(s) is/are best for your household?

It really depends on how many people you're feeding and if you're gone for long periods of time. Here are my recommendations:

For 2–3 person household	3–5 quart slow cooker
For 4–5 person household	5–6 quart slow cooker
For 6+ person household	6½–7 quart slow cooker

Large slow cooker advantages/disadvantages

Advantages:

- You can fit a loaf pan or a baking dish into a 6- or 7-quart, depending on the shape of your cooker. That allows you to make bread or cakes, or even smaller quantities of main dishes. (Take your favorite baking dish and loaf pan along when you shop for a cooker to make sure they'll fit inside.)
- You can feed large groups of people, or make larger quantities of food, allowing for leftovers, or meals, to freeze.

Disadvantages:

- They take up more storage room.
- They don't fit as neatly into a dishwasher.
- If your crock isn't ⅔–¾ full, you may burn your food.

Small slow cooker advantages/disadvantages

Advantages:

- They're great for lots of appetizers, for serving hot drinks, for baking cakes straight in the crock, and for dorm rooms or apartments.
- Great option for making recipes of smaller quantities.

Disadvantages:

- Food in smaller quantities tends to cook more quickly than larger amounts. So keep an eye on it.
- Chances are, you won't have many leftovers. So, if you like to have leftovers, a smaller slow cooker may not be a good option for you.

My recommendation

Have at least two slow cookers; one around 3 to 4 quarts and one 6 quarts or larger. A third would be a huge bonus (and a great advantage to your cooking repertoire!). The advantage of having at least a couple is you can make a larger variety of recipes. Also, you can make at least two or three dishes at once for a whole meal.

Manual vs. Programmable

If you are gone for only six to eight hours a day, a manual slow cooker might be just fine for you. If you are gone for more than eight hours during the day, I would highly recommend purchasing a programmable slow cooker that will switch to warm when the cook time you set is up. It will allow you to cook a wider variety of recipes.

The two I use most frequently are my 4-quart manual slow cooker and my 6½-quart programmable slow cooker. I like that I can make smaller portions in my 4-quart slow cooker on days I don't need or want leftovers, but I also love how my 6½-quart slow cooker can accommodate whole chickens, turkey breasts, hams, or big batches of soups. I use them both often.

Get to Know Your Slow Cooker . . .

Plan a little time to get acquainted with your slow cooker. Each slow cooker has its own personality—just like your oven (and your car). Plus, many new slow cookers cook hotter and faster than earlier models. I think that with all of the concern for food safety, the slow cooker manufacturers have amped up their settings so that "High," "Low," and "Warm" are all higher temperatures than in the older models. That means they cook hotter—and therefore, faster—than the first slow cookers. The beauty of these little machines is that they're supposed to cook low and slow. We count on that when we flip the switch in the morning before we leave the house for ten hours or so. So, because none of us knows what kind of temperament our slow cooker has until we try it out, nor how hot it cooks—don't assume anything. Save yourself a disappointment and make the first recipe in your new slow cooker on a day when you're at home. Cook it for the shortest amount of time the recipe calls for. Then, check the food to see if it's done. Or if you start smelling food that seems to be finished, turn off the cooker and rescue your food.

Also, all slow cookers seem to have a "hot spot," which is of great importance to know, especially when baking with your slow cooker. This spot may tend to burn food in that area if you're not careful. If you're baking directly in your slow cooker, I recommend covering the "hot spot" with some foil.

Take notes . . .

Don't be afraid to make notes in your cookbook. It's yours! Chances are, it will eventually get passed down to someone in your family and they will love and appreciate all of your musings. Take note of which slow cooker you used and exactly how long it took to cook the recipe. The next time you make it, you won't need to try to remember. Apply what you learned to the next recipes you make in your cooker. If another recipe says it needs to cook 7–9 hours, and you've discovered your slow cooker cooks on the faster side, cook that recipe for 6–6½ hours and then check it. You can always cook a recipe longer—but you can't reverse things if it's overdone.

Get creative . . .

If you know your morning is going to be hectic, prepare everything the night before, take it out so the crock warms up to room temperature when you first get up in the morning, then plug it in and turn it on as you're leaving the house.

If you want to make something that has a short cook time and you're going to be gone longer than that, cook it the night before and refrigerate it for the next day. Warm it up when you get home. Or, cook those recipes on the weekend when you know you'll be home and eat them later in the week.

Slow-Cooker Tips and Tricks and Other Things You May Not Know

- Slow cookers tend to work best when they're ⅔ to ¾ of the way full. You may need to increase the cooking time if you've exceeded that amount, or reduce it if you've put in less than that. If you're going to exceed that limit, it would be best to reduce the recipe, or split it between two slow cookers. (Remember how I suggested owning at least two or three slow cookers?)
- Keep your veggies on the bottom. That puts them in more direct contact with the heat. The fuller your slow cooker, the longer it will take its contents to cook. Also, the more densely packed the cooker's contents are, the longer they will take to cook. And finally, the larger the chunks of meat or vegetables, the more time they will need to cook.
- Keep the lid on! Every time you take a peek, you lose 20 minutes of cooking time. Please take this into consideration each time you lift the lid! I know, some of you can't help yourself and are going to lift anyway. Just don't forget to tack on 20 minutes to your cook time for each time you peeked!
- Sometimes it's beneficial to remove the lid. If you'd like your dish to thicken a bit, take the lid off during the last half hour to hour of cooking time.
- If you have a big slow cooker (7- to 8-quart), you can cook a small batch in it by putting the recipe ingredients into an oven-safe baking dish or baking pan and then placing that into the cooker's crock. First, put a trivet or some metal jar rings on the bottom of the

crock, and then set your dish or pan on top of them. Or a loaf pan may "hook onto" the top ridges of the crock belonging to a large oval cooker and hang there straight and securely, "baking" a cake or quick bread. Cover the cooker and flip it on.

- The outside of your slow cooker will be hot! Please remember to keep it out of reach of children and keep that in mind for yourself as well!
- Get yourself a quick-read meat thermometer and use it! This helps remove the question of whether or not your meat is fully cooked, and helps prevent you from overcooking your meat as well.
    - Internal Cooking Temperatures: Beef—125–130°F (rare); 140–145°F (medium); 160°F (well-done)
    - Pork—140–145°F (rare); 145–150°F (medium); 160°F (well-done)
    - Turkey and Chicken—165°F
    - Frozen meat: The basic rule of thumb is, don't put frozen meat into the slow cooker. The meat does not reach the proper internal temperature in time. This especially applies to thick cuts of meat! Proceed with caution!
- Add fresh herbs 10 minutes before the end of the cooking time to maximize their flavor.
- If your recipe calls for cooked pasta, add it 10 minutes before the end of the cooking time if the cooker is on High; 30 minutes before the end of the cooking time if it's on Low. Then the pasta won't get mushy.
- If your recipe calls for sour cream or cream, stir it in 5 minutes before the end of the cooking time. You want it to heat but not boil or simmer.
- Approximate Slow Cooker Temperatures (Remember, each slow cooker is different):
    - High—212°F–300°F
    - Low—170°F–200°F
    - Simmer—185°F
    - Warm—165°F
- Cooked beans freeze well. Store them in freezer bags (squeeze the air out first) or freezer boxes. Cooked and dried bean measurements:
    - 16-oz. can, drained = about 1¾ cups beans
    - 19-oz. can, drained = about 2 cups beans
    - 1 lb. dried beans (about 2½ cups) = 5 cups cooked beans

What Is an Instant Pot?

In short, an Instant Pot is a digital pressure cooker that also has multiple other functions. Not only can it be used as a pressure cooker, but depending on which model Instant Pot you have, you can set it to do things like sauté, cook rice, grains, porridge, soup/stew, beans/chili, porridge, meat, poultry, cake, eggs, yogurt. You can use the Instant Pot to steam or slow cook or even set it manually. Because the Instant Pot has so many functions, it takes away the need for multiple appliances on your counter and allows you to use fewer pots and pans.

Getting Started with Your Instant Pot

Get to Know Your Instant Pot . . .

The very first thing most Instant Pot owners do is called the water test. It helps you get to know your Instant Pot a bit, familiarizes you with it, and might even take a bit of your apprehension away (because if you're anything like me, I was scared to death to use it).

Step 1: Plug in your Instant Pot. This may seem obvious to some, but when we're nervous about using a new appliance, sometimes we forget things like this.
Step 2: Make sure the inner pot is inserted in the cooker. You should *never* attempt to cook anything in your device without the inner pot, or you will ruin your Instant Pot. Food should never come into contact with the actual housing unit.
Step 3: The inner pot has lines for each cup. Fill the inner pot with water until it reaches the 3-cup line.
Step 4: Check the sealing ring to be sure it's secure and in place. You should not be able to move it around. If it's not in place properly, you may experience issues with the pot letting out a lot of steam while cooking, or not coming to pressure.
Step 5: Seal the lid. There is an arrow on the lid between "open" and "close." There is also an arrow on the top of the base of the Instant Pot between a picture of a locked lock and an unlocked lock. Line those arrows up, then turn the lid toward the picture of the lock (left). You will hear a noise that will indicate the lid is locked. If you do not hear a noise, it's not locked. Try it again.
Step 6: *Always* check to see if the steam valve on top of the lid is turned to "sealing." If it's not on "sealing" and is on "venting," it will not be able to come to pressure.
Step 7: Press the "Steam" button and use the +/- arrow to set it to 2 minutes. Once it's at the desired time, you don't need to press anything else. In a few seconds, the Instant Pot will begin all on its own. For those of us with digital slow cookers, we have a tendency to look for the "start" button, but there isn't one on the Instant Pot.
Step 8: Now you wait for the "magic" to happen! The cooking will begin once the device comes to pressure. This can take anywhere from 5 to 30 minutes, in my experience. Then, you will

see the countdown happen (from the time you set it for). After that, the Instant Pot will beep, which means your meal is done!

Step 9: Your Instant Pot will now automatically switch to "warm" and begin a count of how many minutes it's been on warm. The next part is where you either wait for the NPR, or natural pressure release (the pressure releases on its own) or do what's called a QR, or quick release (you manually release the pressure). Which method you choose depends on what you're cooking, but in this case, you can choose either, because it's just water. For NPR, you will wait for the lever to move all the way back over to "venting" and watch the pinion (float valve) next to the lever. It will be flush with the lid when at full pressure and will drop when the pressure is done releasing. If you choose QR, be very careful not to have your hands over the vent, as the steam is very hot and you can burn yourself.

The Three Most Important Buttons You Need to Know About

You will find the majority of recipes will use the following three buttons:

Manual/Pressure Cook: Some older models tend to say "Manual," and the newer models seem to say "Pressure Cook." They mean the same thing. From here, you use the +/- button to change the cook time. After several seconds, the Instant Pot will begin its process. The exact name of this button will vary on your model of Instant Pot.

Sauté: Many recipes will have you sauté vegetables, or brown meat before beginning the pressure cooking process. For this setting, you will not use the lid of the Instant Pot.

Keep Warm/Cancel: This may just be the most important button on the Instant Pot. When you forget to use the +/- buttons to change the time for a recipe, or you press a wrong button, you can hit "keep warm/cancel" and it will turn your Instant Pot off for you.

What Do All the Buttons Do?

With so many buttons, it's hard to remember what each one does or means. You can use this as a quick guide in a pinch.

Soup/Broth. This button cooks at high pressure for 30 minutes. It can be adjusted using the +/- buttons to cook more, for 40 minutes, or less, for 20 minutes.

Meat/Stew. This button cooks at high pressure for 35 minutes. It can be adjusted using the +/- buttons to cook more, for 45 minutes, or less, for 20 minutes.

Bean/Chili. This button cooks at high pressure for 30 minutes. It can be adjusted using the +/- buttons to cook more, for 40 minutes, or less, for 25 minutes.

Poultry. This button cooks at high pressure for 15 minutes. It can be adjusted using the +/- buttons to cook more, for 30 minutes, or less, for 5 minutes.

Rice. This button cooks at low pressure and is the only fully automatic program. It is for cooking white rice and will automatically adjust the cooking time depending on the amount of water and rice in the cooking pot.

Multigrain. This button cooks at high pressure for 40 minutes. It can be adjusted using the +/- buttons to cook more, for 45 minutes of warm water soaking time and 60 minutes pressure cooking time, or less, for 20 minutes.

Porridge. This button cooks at high pressure for 20 minutes. It can be adjusted using the +/- buttons to cook more, for 30 minutes, or less, for 15 minutes.

Steam. This button cooks at high pressure for 10 minutes. It can be adjusted using the +/- buttons to cook more, for 15 minutes, or less, for 3 minutes. Always use a rack or steamer basket with this function, because it heats at full power continuously while it's coming to pressure, and you do not want food in direct contact with the bottom of the pressure cooking pot or it will burn. Once it reaches pressure, the steam button regulates pressure by cycling on and off, similar to the other pressure buttons.

Less | Normal | More. Adjust between the *Less* | *Normal* | *More* settings by pressing the same cooking function button repeatedly until you get to the desired setting. (Older versions use the *Adjust* button.)

+/- Buttons. Adjust the cook time up [+] or down [-]. (On newer models, you can also press and hold [-] or [+] for 3 seconds to turn sound OFF or ON.)

Cake. This button cooks at high pressure for 30 minutes. It can be adjusted using the +/- buttons to cook more, for 40 minutes, or less, for 25 minutes.

Egg. This button cooks at high pressure for 5 minutes. It can be adjusted using the +/- buttons to cook more, for 6 minutes, or less, for 4 minutes.

Instant Pot Tips and Tricks and Other Things You May Not Know

- Never attempt to cook directly in the Instant Pot without the inner pot!
- Once you set the time, you can walk away. It will show the time you set it to, then will change to the word "on" while the pressure builds. Once the Instant Pot has come to pressure, you will once again see the time you set it for. It will count down from there.
- Always make sure the sealing ring is securely in place. If it shows signs of wear or tear, it needs to be replaced.

- Have a sealing ring for savory recipes and a separate sealing ring for sweet recipes. Many people report their desserts tasting like a roast (or another savory food) if they try to use the same sealing ring for all recipes.
- The stainless steel rack (trivet) the Instant Pot comes with can used to keep food from being completely submerged in liquid, like baked potatoes or ground beef. It can also be used to set another pot on, for pot-in-pot cooking.
- If you use warm or hot liquid instead of cold liquid, you may need to adjust the cooking time, or the food may not come out done.
- Always double-check to see that the valve on the lid is set to "sealing" and not "venting" when you first lock the lid. This will save you from the Instant Pot not coming to pressure.
- Use Natural Pressure Release for tougher cuts of meat, recipes with high starch (like rice or grains), and recipes with a high volume of liquid. This means you let the Instant Pot naturally release pressure. The little bobbin will fall once pressure is released completely.
- Use Quick Release for more delicate cuts of meat, such as seafood and chicken breasts, and for steaming vegetables. This means you manually turn the vent (being careful not to put your hand over the vent) to release the pressure. The little bobbin will fall once pressure is released completely.
- Make sure there is a clear pathway for the steam to release. The last thing you want is to ruin the bottom of your cupboards with all that steam.
- You *must* use liquid in the Instant Pot. The *minimum* amount of liquid you should have in the inner pot is ½ cup, but most recipes work best with at least 1 cup.
- Do *not* overfill the Instant Pot! It should only be ½ full for rice or beans (food that expands greatly when cooked,) or ⅔ of the way full for almost everything else. Do not fill it to the max fill line.
- In this book, the Cook Time *does not* take into account the amount of time it will take the Instant Pot to come to pressure, or the amount of time it will take the Instant Pot to release pressure. Be aware of this when choosing a recipe to make.
- If the Instant Pot is not coming to pressure, it's usually because the sealing ring is not on properly, or the vent is not set to "sealing."
- The more liquid, or the colder the ingredients, the longer it will take for the Instant Pot to come to pressure.
- Always make sure that the Instant Pot is dry before inserting the inner pot, and make sure the inner pot is dry before inserting it into the Instant Pot.
- Use a binder clip to hold the inner pot tight against the outer pot when sautéing and stirring. This will keep the pot from "spinning" in the base.

- Doubling a recipe does not change the cook time, but instead it will take longer to come up to pressure.
- You do not always need to double the liquid when doubling a recipe. Depending on what you're making, more liquid may make the food too watery. Use your best judgment.
- When using the slow cooker function, use the following chart:

Slow Cooker	Instant Pot
Warm	Less or Low
Low	Normal or Medium
High	More or High

Instant Pot Accessories

Most Instant Pots come with a stainless steel trivet. Below, you will find a list of common accessories that are frequently used in most Fix-It and Forget-It Instant Pot cookbooks. Most of these accessories can be purchased in-store or online.

- Steamer basket—stainless steel or silicone
- 7-inch nonstick or silicone springform or cake pan
- Sling or trivet with handles
- 1½-quart round baking dish
- Silicone egg molds

Breakfasts

Giant Healthy Pancake

Hope Comerford, Clinton Township, MI

Makes 4 servings
Prep. Time: 10 minutes · *Cooking Time: 17 minutes*

- ¾ cup whole wheat flour
- ¼ cup all-purpose flour
- ¾ tsp. baking powder
- ¾ tsp. baking soda
- 1 large egg
- 1¼ cups unsweetened almond milk
- 1½ Tbsp. unsweetened applesauce
- 1 cup water

Serving suggestion:
Serve with maple syrup, a drizzle of honey, or topped with your favorite fruit.

1. In a bowl, mix the whole wheat flour, all-purpose flour, baking powder, and baking soda.
2. In a smaller bowl, mix the egg, milk, and unsweetened applesauce until well combined. Pour into the dry ingredients and stir until well combined.
3. Spray a 7-inch round springform pan with nonstick cooking spray and then pour the pancake batter into it.
4. Pour the water into the inner pot of the Instant Pot. Place the springform pan on the trivet and carefully lower the trivet into the inner pot.
5. Secure the lid and make sure the vent is set to sealing.
6. Manually set your Instant Pot to Low pressure and set the cook time for 17 minutes.
7. When the cook time is over, manually release the pressure.
8. Remove the lid and carefully lift the trivet out with oven mitts.
9. Remove the cake from the pan and allow to cool for a few minutes before serving and to allow the moisture on the surface of the cake to dry.

Cinnamon Caramel Coffee Cake

Hope Comerford, Clinton Township, MI

Makes 4 servings

Prep. Time: 10 minutes ❧ *Cooking Time: 20 minutes*

Topping:

½ cup all-purpose flour
⅓ cup brown sugar
½ tsp. cinnamon
2 Tbsp. cold butter, chopped
¼ cup chopped pecans, *optional*

Batter:

2 cups all-purpose flour
1 tsp. baking powder
⅓ cup brown sugar
1 tsp. cinnamon
1 tsp. vanilla extract
¼ tsp. salt
2 Tbsp. butter, melted
⅔ cup milk
½ cup caramel bits
1 cup water

1. Spray a 7-inch springform pan with nonstick spray.

2. Mix the flour, brown sugar, cinnamon, and cold butter from the topping list with a fork, pastry cutter, or with clean fingers. Add in the optional chopped pecans if desired.

3. Spread half of the topping in the springform pan. Set the rest aside.

4. Mix the batter ingredients in a bowl and stir until smooth.

5. Pour half the batter into the pan. Sprinkle the remaining topping over the batter, then pour the remaining batter over the top.

6. Cover the pan with foil.

7. Pour the water into the inner pot of the Instant Pot and place the trivet inside. Make sure the handles are up.

8. Place the covered springform pan on top of the trivet.

9. Seal the lid and set the vent to sealing.

10. Manually set the cook time for 20 minutes.

11. When cook time is up, let the pressure release naturally, then carefully remove the lid and pan.

12. Let the cake cool with the foil off before slicing and serving.

Biscuits and Gravy the Instant Pot Way

Hope Comerford, Clinton Township, MI

Makes 4 servings

Prep. Time: 5 minutes ⁂ *Cooking Time: 16–20 minutes*

Gravy:

1 Tbsp. butter

8 oz. bulk breakfast sausage

3 Tbsp. all-purpose flour

½ tsp. garlic powder

¼ tsp. sea salt

¼ tsp. black pepper

1½ cups milk

Biscuits:

¾ cups baking mix

⅓ cup milk

¼ tsp. black pepper

¼ tsp. sea salt

1. Set the Instant Pot to the Sauté setting and place the butter in the inner pot to melt.
2. Add in the breakfast sausage and sauté until browned, about 8 minutes.
3. Stir in the flour, garlic powder, sea salt, and pepper.
4. Whisk in the milk, and bring to a simmer, stirring occasionally.
5. Press Cancel on the Instant Pot.
6. In a bowl, mix the biscuit ingredients.
7. Place dollops of the biscuit mixture over the gravy.
8. Secure the lid and set the vent to sealing.
9. Manually set the cook time for 4 minutes.
10. When cook time is up, let the pressure release naturally for 5 minutes, then manually release the remaining pressure.
11. Serve and enjoy!

Breakfast Burrito Casserole

Hope Comerford, Clinton Township, MI

Makes 6 burritos

Prep. Time: 5–7 minutes *Cooking Time: 13 minutes*

- 1 tsp. olive oil
- 8 oz. ground chorizo
- ⅓ cup chopped onion
- 1 poblano pepper, seeded and diced
- 16 oz. potatoes, peeled and diced
- 1 cup water
- 4 eggs
- ¼ tsp. salt
- ¼ tsp. pepper
- ⅓ cup shredded Mexican blend cheese (or any cheese of your liking)
- ¼ cup of your favorite fresh salsa, *optional*
- 6 flour tortillas

Tip:

You can use frozen diced potatoes if you do not have time to chop fresh potatoes.

1. Set the Instant Pot to the Sauté function and heat the olive oil.
2. Add in the chorizo, onion, and the poblano pepper, and sauté until browned, about 5 minutes.
3. Add in the potatoes and sauté for about 5 minutes longer.
4. Remove the chorizo/potato mix from the inner pot and set aside.
5. Pour 1 cup of water into the inner pot and scrape up any bits on the bottom of the pot.
6. Place the trivet with handles into the inner pot.
7. In a bowl, mix the eggs, salt, and pepper. Stir in the chorizo/potato mix.
8. Spray a 7-inch round baking pan with nonstick spray. Pour the egg/chorizo/potato mix into the pan and sprinkle with the cheese. Cover with foil.
9. Place the pan on top of the trivet. Secure the lid and set the vent to sealing.
10. Manually set the cook time for 13 minutes on high pressure.
11. When cook time is up, let the pressure release naturally.
12. When the pin drops, remove the lid and then carefully remove the baking pan from the trivet.
13. Fill the tortillas with some of the filling and wrap up like a burrito.

Fiesta Hashbrowns

Dena Mell-Dorchy, Royal Oak, MI

Makes 8 servings

Prep. Time: 15 minutes ❧ *Cooking Time: 8–9 hours* ❧ *Ideal slow-cooker size: 3- or 4-qt.*

- 1 lb. ground turkey sausage
- ½ cup chopped onion
- 5 cups potatoes, peeled and diced
- 8 oz. chicken stock
- 1 small red sweet pepper
- 1 jalapeño pepper, seeded and finely diced
- 1½ cups sliced mushrooms
- 2 Tbsp. quick-cooking tapioca
- ½ cup shredded Monterey Jack cheese

1. Spray slow cooker with nonstick spray.
2. In a large skillet, brown sausage and onion over medium heat. Drain off fat.
3. Combine sausage mixture, potatoes, chicken stock, sweet pepper, jalapeño, mushrooms, and quick-cooking tapioca in cooker; stir to combine.
4. Cover and cook on Low for 8–9 hours. Stir before serving. Top with shredded Monterey Jack cheese.

Tip:

You can use frozen diced potatoes if you do not have time to chop fresh potatoes.

Spinach Frittata

Shirley Unternahrer, Wayland, IA

Makes 4–6 servings

Prep. Time: 15 minutes ❧ *Cooking Time: 1½–2 hours* ❧ *Ideal slow-cooker size: 5-qt.*

- 4 eggs
- ½ tsp. kosher salt
- ½ tsp. dried basil
- Fresh ground pepper to taste
- 3 cups chopped fresh spinach, stems removed
- ½ cup chopped tomato, liquid drained off
- ⅓ cup freshly grated Parmesan cheese

1. Whisk eggs well in mixing bowl. Whisk in salt, basil, and pepper.
2. Gently stir in spinach, tomato, and Parmesan.
3. Pour into lightly greased slow cooker.
4. Cover and cook on High for 1½–2 hours, until middle is set. Serve hot.

Spinach and Mushroom Frittata

J. B. Miller, Indianapolis, IN

Makes 4 servings

Prep. Time: 5 minutes · *Cooking Time: 10 minutes*

6 eggs
½ tsp. salt
¼ tsp. black pepper
1 Tbsp. fresh basil, minced
3 cloves garlic, minced
1 small shallot, minced
½ lb. sliced baby bella mushrooms
10-ounce bag fresh spinach
¼ cup shredded Gruyère cheese
1 cup water

1. In a bowl, beat the eggs, salt, and pepper.
2. Gently fold in the basil, garlic, shallot, mushrooms, spinach, and cheese.
3. Spray a 7-inch round pan with nonstick cooking spray, then pour in the egg/vegetable/cheese mixture.
4. Pour the water into the bottom of the inner pot of the Instant Pot.
5. Place the 7-inch round pan on top of the trivet and slowly lower it into the Instant Pot using the handles.
6. Secure the lid and set the valve to sealing.
7. Set the Instant Pot to Manual and set the cooking time to 10 minutes.
8. When the cooking time is over, let the pressure release naturally, then remove the lid and remove the trivet and pan carefully with oven mitts.
9. Slice into 4 slices and serve warm.

Italian Frittata

Hope Comerford, Clinton Township, MI

Makes 6 servings

Prep. Time: 10 minutes · *Cooking Time: 3–4 hours* · *Ideal slow-cooker size: 5- or 6-qt.*

10 eggs
1 Tbsp. chopped fresh basil
1 Tbsp. chopped fresh mint
1 Tbsp. chopped fresh sage
1 Tbsp. chopped fresh oregano
½ tsp. sea salt
⅛ tsp. pepper
1 Tbsp. grated Parmesan cheese
¼ cup diced prosciutto
½ cup chopped onion

1. Spray your crock with nonstick spray.
2. In a bowl, mix the eggs, basil, mint, sage, oregano, sea salt, pepper, and Parmesan. Pour this mixture into the crock.
3. Sprinkle the prosciutto and onion evenly over the egg mixture in the crock.
4. Cover and cook on Low for 3–4 hours.

Easy Quiche

Becky Bontrager Horst, Goshen, IN

Makes 6 servings, 1 slice per serving

Prep. Time: 15 minutes ❧ *Cooking Time: 25 minutes*

- 1 cup water
- ¼ cup chopped onion
- ¼ cup chopped mushrooms, *optional*
- 3 oz. shredded cheddar cheese
- 2 Tbsp. bacon bits, chopped ham, or browned sausage
- 4 eggs
- ¼ tsp. salt
- 1½ cups milk
- ½ cup whole wheat flour
- 1 Tbsp. soft margarine

1. Pour the water into the inner pot of the Instant Pot and place the steaming rack inside.
2. Spray a 7-inch round baking pan with nonstick cooking spray.
3. Sprinkle the onion, mushrooms, shredded cheddar, and meat in the cake pan.
4. In a medium bowl, combine the remaining ingredients. Pour them over the meat and vegetables.
5. Place the baking pan onto the steaming rack, close the lid, and secure to the locking position. Be sure the vent is turned to sealing. Set for 25 minutes on Manual at high pressure.
6. Let the pressure release naturally.
7. Carefully remove the cake pan with the handles of the steaming rack and allow to stand for 10 minutes before cutting and serving.

Spanish Breakfast "Skillet"

Hope Comerford, Clinton Township, MI

Makes 6 servings

Prep. Time: 25 minutes ∘ *Cooking Time: 5–6 hours* ∘ *Ideal slow-cooker size: 5- or 6-qt.*

- 1 lb. turkey sausage, browned, drained
- 4.5-oz. pkg. tostada shells, broken coarsely
- 1 medium red bell pepper, chopped
- 1 medium onion, chopped
- 4-oz. can diced green chilies
- 1 cup almond milk
- 12 eggs
- 1 tsp. sea salt
- ¼ tsp. black pepper
- ½ cup crumbled queso fresco
- Optional toppings: 2 sliced avocados, 8 oz. non-fat Greek yogurt, 2 cups salsa

1. Spray crock with nonstick spray.
2. In crock, combine browned sausage, tostada pieces, red bell pepper, onion, and green chilies.
3. In a large bowl, mix the almond milk, eggs, sea salt, and black pepper.
4. Pour egg mixture over sausage mixture in crock.
5. Sprinkle crumbled queso fresco over the top.
6. Cover and cook on Low for 5–6 hours.

Egg Bites

Hope Comerford, Clinton Township, MI

Makes 14 mini quiches

Prep. Time: 15 minutes ⁂ *Cooking Time: 11 minutes* ⁂ *Cooling Time: 5 minutes*

2 tsp. olive oil
½ green bell pepper, diced
¼ cup finely chopped broccoli florets
½ small onion, diced
5 oz. fresh spinach
8 eggs
¼ cup nonfat milk
3 drops hot sauce, *optional*
⅓ cup shredded cheddar cheese
1 cup water

1. In a small pan on the stove, heat the olive oil over medium-high heat. Sauté the bell pepper, broccoli, and onion for about 8 minutes. Add the spinach and continue to cook until wilted.
2. Spray 2 egg molds with nonstick cooking spray. Divide the cooked vegetables evenly between the egg bite mold cups.
3. In a bowl, whisk the eggs, milk, and hot sauce (if using). Divide this evenly between the egg bite mold cups, or until each cup is ⅔ of the way full.
4. Evenly divide the shredded cheese between the cups. Cover them tightly with foil.
5. Pour the water into the inner pot of the Instant Pot. Place the trivet on top, then place the 2 filled egg bite molds on top of the trivet, the top one stacked on top of the one below.
6. Secure the lid and set the vent to sealing.
7. Manually set the cook time for 11 minutes on high pressure.
8. When the cook time is up, let the pressure release naturally for 5 minutes, then manually release the remaining pressure.
9. When the pin drops, remove the lid and carefully lift the trivet and molds out with oven mitts.
10. Place the molds on a wire rack and uncover. Let cool for about 5 minutes, then pop them out onto a plate or serving platter.

Serving suggestion:

Serve alongside some freshly baked bread and a bowl of fruit.

Delicious Shirred Eggs

Hope Comerford, Clinton Township, MI

Makes 6 servings

Prep. Time: 5 minutes · *Cooking Time: 2–3 minutes*

1 clove garlic, minced
2 Tbsp. fresh minced onion
6 Tbsp. milk, *divided*
6 jumbo eggs
6 Tbsp. grated fresh Parmesan cheese, *divided*
Fresh cracked pepper
1 cup water

1. Spray 6 ramekins with nonstick cooking spray.
2. Evenly divide the minced garlic and onion among the 6 ramekins.
3. Pour 1 Tbsp. of milk into each ramekin.
4. Break an egg into each ramekin.
5. Top each egg with 1 Tbsp. freshly grated cheese.
6. Season with fresh cracked pepper.
7. Pour the water into the inner pot of the Instant Pot. Place the trivet on top.
8. Arrange 3 ramekins on top of the trivet, then carefully stack the remaining 3 ramekins on top, staggering their positions so each ramekin on top is sitting between 2 on the bottom layer.
9. Secure the lid and set the vent to sealing.
10. Set the Instant Pot to low pressure and manually set the cook time to 2 minutes for runny yolks or 3 minutes for hard yolks.
11. When cook time is complete, manually release the pressure and remove the lid. Serve immediately.

Apple Oatmeal

Frances B. Musser, Newmanstown, PA

Makes 5 servings

Prep. Time: 20 minutes ❧ *Cooking Time: 3–5 hours* ❧ *Ideal slow-cooker size: 3-qt.*

- 2 cups milk
- 1 cup water
- 1 Tbsp. honey
- 1 Tbsp. coconut oil
- ¼ tsp. kosher salt
- ½ tsp. cinnamon
- 1 cup steel-cut oats
- 1 cup chopped apples
- ½ cup chopped walnuts
- 1 Tbsp. turbinado sugar

1. Grease the inside of the slow-cooker crock.
2. Add all ingredients to crock and mix.
3. Cover. Cook on Low 3–5 hours.

Apple Granola

Phyllis Good, Lancaster, PA

Makes 12 servings
Prep. Time: 20 minutes · *Cooking Time: 2–3 hours*
Cooling time: 1 hour · *Ideal slow-cooker size: 5-qt.*

9 cups unpeeled, sliced apples
1½ tsp. cinnamon
1½ cups dry rolled oats
1½ cups wheat germ
1½ cups whole wheat flour
1½ cups sunflower seeds
1⅓ cups water
¾ cup honey

1. Grease interior of slow-cooker crock.
2. Use your food processor to slice the apples. Place slices in slow cooker.
3. Sprinkle apple slices with cinnamon, and then stir together gently.
4. In a good-sized bowl, stir together dry oats, wheat germ, whole wheat flour, and sunflower seeds.
5. When dry ingredients are well mixed, pour in water and honey. Using a sturdy spoon or your clean hands, mix thoroughly until wet ingredients are damp throughout.
6. Spoon over apples.
7. Cover, but vent the lid by propping it open with a chopstick or wooden spoon handle. Or if you're using an oval cooker, turn the lid sideways.
8. Cook on High for 1 hour, stirring up from the bottom and around the sides every 20 minutes or so. (Set a timer so you don't forget!)
9. Switch the cooker to Low. Bake another 1–2 hours, still stirring every 20 minutes or so.
10. Granola is done when it eventually browns a bit and looks dry.
11. Pour granola onto parchment or a large baking sheet to cool and crisp up more.
12. If you like clumps, no need to stir granola further while it cools. Otherwise, break up the granola with a spoon or your hands as it cools.
13. When completely cooled, store in airtight container.

Pumpkin Breakfast Custard

Audrey Hess, Gettysburg, PA

Makes 4–6 servings

Prep. Time: 20 minutes · Cooking Time: 1½–2 hours · Ideal slow-cooker size: 2½- or 3-qt.

- 2½ cups cooked, peeled, and pureed pumpkin or winter squash
- 2 Tbsp. blackstrap molasses
- 3 Tbsp. maple syrup
- ¼ cup half-and-half
- 3 eggs
- 1 tsp. cinnamon
- ½ tsp. ground ginger
- ½ tsp. ground nutmeg
- ¼ tsp. ground cloves
- ¼ tsp. salt

1. Puree ingredients in blender until smooth.
2. Pour into greased slow cooker.
3. Cook on High for 1½–2 hours, until set in the middle and just browning at edges.
4. Serve warm in scoops over hot cereal, baked oatmeal, or as a breakfast side dish with toast or muffins.

Tip:

If you do not have time for fresh pumpkin or winter squash, you can use canned.

Soups & Stews

Chicken & Turkey

Chicken and Vegetable Soup

Hope Comerford, Clinton Township, MI

Makes 4–6 servings

Prep. Time: 15 minutes ❧ *Cooking Time: 7–8 hours* ❧ *Ideal slow-cooker size: 5-qt.*

- 1 lb. boneless skinless chicken, cut into bite-sized pieces
- 2 celery ribs, diced
- 1 small yellow squash, diced
- 4 oz. sliced mushrooms
- 2 large carrots, diced
- 1 medium onion, chopped
- 8 cloves garlic, minced
- 1 Tbsp. onion powder
- ½ tsp. no-salt seasoning
- 1 tsp. salt
- Black pepper to taste
- 32 oz. chicken stock
- 1 Tbsp. fresh chopped basil

1. Place the chicken, vegetables, and spices (except the basil) into the crock. Pour the chicken stock over the top.

2. Cover and cook on Low for 7–8 hours, or until vegetables are tender. Stir in the fresh basil.

Instant Pot Adaptation:

1. Set the Instant Pot to the "Sauté" function and heat up 1 Tbsp. of olive oil.

2. Sauté the celery, squash, mushrooms, carrots, onion, and garlic for about 5–7 minutes.

3. Pour in 1 cup of the stock and scrape any bits off the bottom of the inner pot. Press "Cancel."

4. Add in the chicken, garlic powder, onion powder, no-salt seasoning, salt, pepper, and remaining stock.

5. Secure the lid and set the vent to "Sealing."

6. Manually set the Instant Pot to cook for 10 minutes on high pressure.

7. When cook time is up, manually release the pressure and remove the lid when the pin drops. Stir in the basil. Serve and enjoy!

Chicken and Vegetable Soup with Rice

Hope Comerford, Clinton Township, MI

Makes 6–8 servings

Prep. Time: 20 minutes ⁂ *Cooking Time: 6½–7½ hours* ⁂ *Ideal slow-cooker size: 3-qt.*

1½–2 lb. boneless, skinless chicken breasts
1½ cups chopped carrots
1½ cups chopped red onion
8 cloves garlic, minced
1 Tbsp. onion powder
1 tsp. salt
¼ tsp. celery seed
¼ tsp. paprika
⅛ tsp. pepper
1 dried bay leaf
8 cups chicken stock
1 cup fresh green beans
3 cups cooked rice

1. Place chicken into the bottom of crock, then add rest of the remaining ingredients, except green beans and rice.

2. Cover and cook on Low for 6–7 hours.

3. Remove chicken and chop into bite-sized cubes. Place chicken back into crock and add in green beans. Cover and cook another 30 minutes.

4. To serve, place approximately ½ cup of the cooked rice into each bowl and ladle soup over top of the rice.

Chicken Noodle Soup

Colleen Heatwole, Burton, MI

Makes 6–8 servings
Prep. Time: 15 minutes *Cooking Time: 4 minutes*

2 Tbsp. butter
1 Tbsp. oil
1 medium onion, diced
3 cloves garlic, minced
2 large carrots, diced
3 celery stalks, diced
Salt to taste
8 cups chicken broth
2 cups cubed cooked chicken
8 oz. medium egg noodles
1 cup peas (if frozen, thaw while preparing soup)
Pepper to taste
3 tsp. chopped fresh thyme
3 tsp. chopped fresh oregano
3 tsp. chopped fresh basil

1. In the inner pot of the Instant Pot, melt the butter with oil on the Sauté function.

2. Add the onion, garlic, carrots, and celery with a large pinch of salt and continue cooking on Sauté until soft, about 5 minutes, stirring frequently.

3. Add the broth, cooked chicken, and noodles, stirring to combine all ingredients.

5. Put the lid on the Instant Pot and set the vent to sealing. Manually set the cook time for 4 minutes on high pressure.

6. When time is up, manually release the pressure.

7. When the pin drops, remove the lid and add the peas, pepper, thyme, oregano and basil. Stir, and adjust seasoning as needed.

Chicken Cheddar Broccoli Soup

Maria Shevlin, Sicklerville, NJ

Makes 4–6 servings
Prep. Time: 15 minutes *Cooking Time: 15 minutes*

1 lb. raw chicken breast, thinly chopped/sliced
1 lb. fresh broccoli, chopped
½ cup chopped onion
2 cloves garlic, minced
1 cup shredded carrots
½ cup finely chopped celery
¼ cup finely chopped red bell pepper
3 cups low-sodium chicken bone broth
½ tsp. salt
¼ tsp. black pepper
Pinch red pepper flakes
2 cups evaporated skim milk
8 oz. freshly shredded cheddar cheese
2 Tbsp. Frank's RedHot Original Cayenne Pepper Sauce
3 tsp. chopped fresh parsley

1. Place chicken, broccoli, chopped onion, garlic, carrots, celery, bell pepper, chicken broth, salt, pepper, and red pepper flakes into the pot and stir.
2. Secure the lid and make sure vent is at sealing. Manually set the cook time for 15 minutes on high pressure.
3. Manually release the pressure when cook time is up. Remove the lid, and stir in evaporated milk.
4. Place pot on sauté setting until it all comes to a low boil, approximately 5 minutes.
5. Stir in cheese, hot sauce, and parsley.
6. Turn off the pot by pressing Cancel. Continue to stir until the cheese is melted.

Serving suggestion:

Serve it up with a slice or two of freshly baked whole grain bread.

Chicken Chili Pepper Stew

Susan Kasting, Jenks, OK

Makes 4 servings

Prep. Time: 5 minutes *Cooking Time: 8 minutes*

14½ oz. low-sodium chicken stock
1 lb. boneless, skinless chicken breasts,
4 cloves garlic, minced
1–2 jalapeño peppers, seeded and diced
1 medium red bell pepper, diced
1 medium carrot, sliced
2 cups fresh corn kernels
1 tsp. cumin
2 Tbsp. chopped cilantro

1. Place all the ingredients, except the chopped cilantro, into the inner pot of the Instant Pot and secure the lid. Set the vent to sealing.
2. Manually set the cook time for 8 minutes on high pressure.
3. When the cooking time is over, let the pressure release naturally for 5 minutes, then manually release the pressure.
4. When the pin drops, remove the lid, remove the chicken, shred between 2 forks, then replace back in the inner pot. Stir.
5. Serve each bowl of stew with a sprinkling of chopped cilantro.

Slow-Cooker Adaptation:

1. In a 6–7 qt. slow cooker, place all the ingredients, except the cilantro.
2. Cover and cook on Low for 7 hours, or High for 3½ hours.
3. Remove the chicken, shred between 2 forks, then replace back in the crock and stir.
4. Serve each bowl of stew with a sprinkling of chopped cilantro.

Spicy Chicken Soup with Edamame

J. B. Miller, Indianapolis, IN

Makes 8 servings

Prep. Time: 8 minutes *Cooking Time: 20 minutes*

2 Tbsp. olive oil
1 bunch (about 6) scallions, thinly sliced
1 red bell pepper, chopped
1 yellow bell pepper, chopped
2 jalapeño peppers, seeded and finely chopped
4 cloves garlic, chopped
1½ lb. boneless, skinless, chicken breasts
½ tsp. ground ginger
½ tsp. ground pepper
4 cups low-sodium chicken broth
3 cups fresh edamame, shelled

1. Set the Instant Pot to Sauté and heat up the oil in the inner pot.

2. Sauté the scallions, bell peppers, jalapeños, and garlic in the oil for about 3 minutes. Push them to the outer edges and sear the chicken breasts on both sides.

3. Press Cancel. Add the remaining ingredients, except for the edamame, and secure the lid. Make sure the vent is set to sealing.

4. Manually set the cook time for 15 minutes on high pressure.

5. When the cooking time is over, manually release the pressure.

6. When the pin drops, remove the lid, then remove the chicken and shred it between 2 forks. Replace it back in the soup.

7. Stir the edamame into the soup and press Keep Warm. Allow it to cook for about 5 additional minutes, then serve.

Tip:

If you don't have time for fresh edamame, or cannot find it, you can use frozen.

Slow-Cooker Adaptation:

1. In a 5–6 qt. slow cooker, place all ingredients, except the edamame.

2. Cover and cook on Low for 7 hours, or on High for 3½ hours.

3. Remove the chicken and shred it between 2 forks. Replace it back in the soup.

4. Stir the edamame into the soup and switch the slow cooker to warm. Cover and allow the soup to cook for about 5 additional minutes, then serve.

Turkey Soup

Joyce Zuercher, Hesston, KS

Makes 6–8 servings

Prep. Time: 40 minutes · *Cooking Time: 3–4 hours* · *Ideal slow-cooker size: 6-qt.*

- 2–3 cups cooked and cut-up turkey
- 3 qt. turkey or chicken broth
- 1 onion, diced
- ½–¾ tsp. salt, or to taste
- 2 cups diced tomatoes
- 1 Tbsp. low-sodium chicken bouillon granules
- ⅛ tsp. pepper
- 4 cups chopped fresh vegetables—any combination of sliced celery, carrots, onions, rutabaga, broccoli, cauliflower, mushrooms, and more
- 1½ cups uncooked noodles
- 3 tsp. chopped fresh thyme
- 4 tsp. chopped fresh oregano

1. Place turkey, broth, onion, salt, tomatoes, bouillon granules, pepper, and vegetables into slow cooker. Stir.

2. Cover. Cook on Low 3–4 hours, or until vegetables are nearly done.

3. Fifteen to 30 minutes before serving time, stir in noodles. Cover. Cook on Low. If noodles are thin and small, they'll cook in 15 minutes or less. If heavier, they may need 30 minutes to become tender.

4. Stir in the fresh thyme and oregano before serving.

Note:

If you've got a big turkey frame, and you know it's got some good meaty morsels on it, here's what to do: Break it up enough to fit into your Dutch oven. Add 3 qt. water, 1 onion, quartered, and 2 tsp. salt. Cover, and simmer 1½ hours. Remove turkey bones from Dutch oven and allow to cool. Then debone and chop meat coarsely. Discard bones and skin. Strain broth. Begin with Step 1 above!

Unstuffed Cabbage Soup

Colleen Heatwole, Burton, MI

Makes 4–6 servings

Prep. Time: 15 minutes · *Cooking Time: 20 minutes*

2 Tbsp. olive oil
1 lb. ground turkey
1 medium onion, diced
2 cloves garlic, minced
1 small head cabbage, chopped, cored, cut into roughly 2-inch pieces.
6 oz. tomato paste
4 cups diced tomatoes, with liquid
2 cups vegetable broth
1½ cups water
¾ cup brown rice
1–2 tsp. salt
½ tsp. black pepper
3 tsp. chopped fresh oregano
3 tsp. chopped fresh parsley

1. Heat the olive oil in the inner pot of the Instant Pot using sauté function. Add ground turkey. Stir frequently for about 2 minutes.

2. Add onion and garlic and continue to sauté for 2 more minutes, stirring frequently.

3. Add chopped cabbage.

4. On top of cabbage, layer tomato paste, tomatoes with liquid, vegetable broth, water, rice, salt, and pepper.

5. Secure the lid and set vent to sealing. Using manual setting, select 20 minutes.

6. When time is up, let the pressure release naturally for 10 minutes, then do a quick release. Stir in the oregano and parsley.

Turkey Meatball Soup

Mary Ann Lefever, Lancaster, PA

Makes 8 servings

Prep. Time: 30 minutes · *Cooking Time: 8 hours* · *Ideal slow-cooker size: 5- or 6-qt.*

- 4–5 large carrots, chopped
- 10 cups chicken broth
- ¾ lb. escarole, washed and cut into bite-sized pieces
- 1 lb. lean ground turkey, uncooked
- 1 medium onion, chopped
- 2 large eggs, beaten
- ½ cup breadcrumbs
- ½ cup freshly grated Parmesan, plus more for serving
- 1 tsp. salt
- ¼ tsp. pepper

1. In slow cooker, combine carrots and broth.
2. Stir in escarole.
3. Cover. Cook on Low 4 hours.
4. Combine turkey, onion, eggs, breadcrumbs, ½ cup Parmesan cheese, salt, and pepper in good-sized bowl. Mix well and shape into 1-inch balls. Drop carefully into soup.
5. Cover cooker. Cook on Low 4 more hours, or just until meatballs and vegetables are cooked through.
6. Serve hot, sprinkled with extra Parmesan cheese.

Variation:

If you wish, you can substitute 3 cups cut-up cooked turkey for the ground turkey meatballs.

Turkey Sausage and Cabbage Soup

Hope Comerford, Clinton Township, MI

Makes 8 servings

Prep. Time: 5 minutes ♣ *Cooking Time: 17 minutes*

- 2 Tbsp. olive oil
- 1½ cups chopped onions
- 2 cloves garlic, finely chopped
- 3 carrots, chopped in rounds
- 1 lb. bulk Italian turkey sausage, removed from casing
- 1 medium head green cabbage, shredded
- 3½ cups diced tomatoes
- ¼ tsp. black pepper
- 32 oz. chicken or vegetable stock
- 4 tsp. chopped fresh oregano
- 3 Tbsp. chopped fresh basil

1. Set the Instant Pot to Sauté and heat the olive oil in the inner pot.
2. Sauté the onions, garlic, and carrots for 2 minutes, then push them to the outer edges and add the sausage. Brown the sausage for about 3 minutes. Press Cancel.
3. Add the cabbage, tomatoes, and black pepper. Finally, pour in the stock.
4. Secure the lid and set the vent to sealing.
5. Manually cook for 17 minutes on high pressure.
6. When the cooking time is over, manually release the pressure. Stir in the oregano and basil. Serve and enjoy!

Slow-Cooker Adaptation:

1. Brown the sausage in pan on the stove. Drain the grease.
2. In a 7-qt slow cooker, add the browned sausage and remaining ingredients, except the oregano and basil, to the slow-cooker crock.
3. Cover and cook on Low for 7 hours, or High for 3½ hours.
4. When cooking time is over, stir in the oregano and basil. Serve and enjoy!

Pork

Shredded Pork Tortilla Soup

Hope Comerford, Clinton Township, MI

Makes 6–8 servings

Prep. Time: 10 minutes ⁂ *Cooking Time: 8–10 hours* ⁂ *Ideal slow-cooker size: 5-qt.*

3 large tomatoes, chopped
1 cup chopped red onion
1 jalapeño pepper, seeded and minced
1-lb. pork loin
2 tsp. cumin
2 tsp. chili powder
2 tsp. onion powder
2 tsp. garlic powder
2 tsp. lime juice
8 cups low-sodium chicken stock

Garnish, *optional*:

Fresh chopped cilantro
Tortilla chips
Avocado slices
Freshly grated Mexican cheese

1. In your crock, place the tomatoes, onion, and jalapeño.

2. Place the pork loin on top.

3. Add all the seasonings and lime juice, then pour in the chicken stock.

4. Cover and cook on Low for 8–10 hours.

5. Remove the pork and shred it between two forks. Place it back into the soup and stir.

6. Serve each bowl of soup with fresh chopped cilantro, tortilla chips, avocado slices, and freshly grated Mexican cheese, if desired . . . or any other garnishes you would like!

Instant Pot Adaptation:

1. Cut the pork loin into several pieces.

2. Place the pork loin, tomatoes, red onion, jalapeño, cumin, chili powder, onion powder, garlic powder, lime juice, and chicken stock into the inner pot of the Instant Pot.

3. Secure the lid and set the vent to sealing. Manually set the cook time for 27 minutes.

4. When cook time is up, let the pressure release naturally for 15 minutes, then manually release any remaining pressure. Once the pin has dropped, remove the lid.

5. Remove the pork pieces and shred between two forks. Place it back into the soup and stir.

6. Serve each bowl of soup with fresh chopped cilantro, tortilla chips, avocado slices, and freshly grated Mexican cheese, if desired . . . or any other garnishes you would like!

Italian Shredded Pork Stew

Emily Fox, Bernville, PA

Makes: 6–8 servings

Prep. Time: 20 minutes · *Cooking Time: 10 hours* · *Ideal slow-cooker size: 5-qt.*

- 2 medium sweet potatoes, peeled and cubed
- 2 cups chopped fresh kale
- 1 large onion, chopped
- 3 cloves garlic, minced
- 2½–3½-lb. boneless pork shoulder butt roast
- ½ cup cannellini beans, soaked overnight, rinsed
- 1½ tsp. Italian seasoning
- ½ tsp. salt
- ½ tsp. pepper
- 5½ cups chicken broth
- Sour cream, *optional*

1. Place sweet potatoes, kale, onion, and garlic in slow cooker.
2. Place roast on vegetables.
3. Add beans and seasonings.
4. Pour the broth over the other ingredients.
5. Cover and cook on Low for 10 hours or until meat is tender.
6. Remove meat. Skim fat from cooking juices if desired. Shred pork with 2 forks and return to cooker. Heat through.
7. Garnish with sour cream if desired.

The Best Bean and Ham Soup

Hope Comerford, Clinton Township, MI

Makes 8–10 servings

Prep. Time: 10 minutes ⁂ *Soaking Time: 12–24 hours* ⁂ *Cooking Time: 40 minutes*

1 Tbsp. olive oil
1 cup chopped onions
2 cloves garlic, minced
1 cup chopped celery
8–10 cups water, *divided*
1 meaty ham bone or shank
1 lb. dry navy beans, soaked overnight, rinsed
¼ cup chopped parsley
1 Tbsp. salt
1 tsp. pepper
1 tsp. nutmeg
1 tsp. oregano
1 tsp. basil
1 bay leaf
1 cup mashed potato flakes

1. Set the Instant Pot to Sauté and add in the olive oil to heat.

2. Sauté the onions, garlic, and celery for 5 minutes.

3. Pour in 1 cup of water and scrape any bits off the bottom of the Inner Pot. Press Cancel.

4. Place the ham bone in inner pot, then pour in all the remaining ingredients except mashed potato flakes.

5. Fill with the remaining water, or until ⅔ of the way full.

6. Secure the lid and set the vent to sealing. Manually set the cook time for 35 minutes on high pressure.

7. When cook time is up, let the pressure release naturally.

8. When the pin drops, carefully remove the lid. Remove the bay leaf and ham bone/cartilage. Stir in the mashed potato flakes. Let the soup thicken for a few minutes, then serve.

Slow-Cooker Adaptation:

1. In a 7- or 8-quart slow cooker, place the ham bone in the bottom of the crock and pour all the remaining ingredients, except the mashed potato flakes, into the crock around it, ending with enough water to make sure you've covered the ham bone with water (approx. 8 cups).

2. Cover and cook on Low for 10–12 hours.

3. When the cook time is over, remove the bay leaf and ham bone/cartilage. Stir in the mashed potato flakes. Let the soup thicken for a few minutes, then serve.

Split Pea Soup

Judy Gascho, Woodburn, OR

Makes 3–4 servings

Prep. Time: 20 minutes *Cooking Time: 15 minutes*

- 4 cups chicken broth
- 4 sprigs thyme
- 4 oz. ham, diced (about ⅓ cup)
- 2 Tbsp. butter
- 2 stalks celery
- 2 carrots
- 1 large leek
- 3 cloves garlic
- 1 cup dried green split peas (about 12 oz.)
- Salt and pepper to taste

1. Pour the broth into the inner pot of the Instant Pot and set to Sauté. Add the thyme, ham, and butter.

2. While the broth heats, chop the celery and cut the carrots into ½-inch-thick rounds. Halve the leek lengthwise and thinly slice and chop the garlic. Add the vegetables to the pot as you cut them. Rinse the split peas in a colander, discarding any stones, then add to the pot.

3. Secure the lid, making sure the steam valve is in the sealing position. Set the cooker to Manual at high pressure for 15 minutes. When the time is up, carefully turn the steam valve to the venting position to release the pressure manually.

4. Turn off the Instant Pot. Remove the lid and stir the soup; discard the thyme sprigs.

5. Thin the soup with up to 1 cup of water if needed (the soup will continue to thicken as it cools). Season with salt and pepper.

Beef & Lamb

Beef Mushroom Barley Soup

Becky Frey, Lebanon, PA

Makes 8 servings

Prep. Time: 20 minutes · *Cooking Time: 25 minutes*

2 Tbsp. olive oil, *divided*
1 lb. boneless beef chuck, cubed
1 large onion, chopped
2 cloves garlic, crushed
1 lb. fresh mushrooms, sliced
1 celery rib, sliced
2 carrots, sliced
8 cups beef stock
½ cup uncooked pearl barley
½ tsp. freshly ground pepper
1½ tsp. chopped fresh thyme, *optional*
3 Tbsp. chopped fresh parsley

1. Set the Instant Pot to the Sauté function and heat 1 Tbsp. of the olive oil in the inner pot.
2. Brown the beef, in batches if needed, and then remove and set aside.
3. Add the remaining Tbsp. of olive oil and sauté the onion, garlic, and mushrooms for 3 to 4 minutes.
4. Add the beef back in, as well as all the remaining ingredients, except for the thyme and parsley. Press Cancel.
5. Secure the lid and set the vent to sealing.
6. Manually set the cook time to 25 minutes on high pressure.
7. When the cooking time is over, let the pressure release naturally for 15 minutes, then manually release the remaining pressure.
8. When the pin drops, remove the lid and stir in the optional thyme. Serve each bowl topped with some fresh chopped parsley.

Colorful Beef Stew

Hope Comerford, Clinton Township, MI

Makes 6 servings

Prep. Time: 20 minutes · *Cooking Time: 8–9 hours* · *Ideal slow-cooker size: 4-qt.*

- 2 lb. boneless beef chuck roast, trimmed of fat and cut into ¾-inch pieces
- 1 large red onion, chopped
- 2 cups beef broth
- 6 oz. tomato paste
- 4 cloves garlic, minced
- 1 Tbsp. paprika
- 2 tsp. dried marjoram
- ½ tsp. black pepper
- 1 tsp. sea salt
- 1 red bell pepper, seeded and sliced
- 1 yellow bell pepper, seeded and sliced
- 1 orange bell pepper, seeded and sliced

1. Place all ingredients in the crock, except the sliced bell peppers, and stir.

2. Cover and cook on Low for 8–9 hours. Stir in sliced bell peppers during the last 45 minutes of cooking time.

Moroccan Spiced Stew

Melissa Paskvan, Novi, MI

Makes 6–8 servings

Prep. Time: 10 minutes · *Cooking Time: 8 hours* · *Ideal slow-cooker size: 5-qt.*

3 cups chopped tomatoes
3 cups chicken stock
1 lb. lamb (ground or stew-cut pieces)
1 medium onion, chopped
⅛ tsp. fresh grated ginger
1½ tsp. cumin
¾ tsp. cinnamon
¾ tsp. turmeric
⅛–¼ tsp. cayenne pepper
½ cup shredded or chopped carrots
3 cups chopped sweet potato
Salt and pepper to taste

1. Place all ingredients in the crock and mix well to incorporate the spices.

2. Cover and cook on Low for 8 hours.

Serving suggestion:

Top with harissa for a zesty, warm flavor. Ladle this stew over brown rice or millet for a filling meal. Cook with ½ cup dried apricots or dates to impart a sweet taste.

Tip:

If you really want to seal in the warm spices, add 1 Tbsp. olive oil to a pan and brown just the outsides of the lamb pieces and cook with onions and spices. Then add in about 1 cup of the chicken stock to deglaze the pan and pour all ingredients from the pan to the slow cooker then add the remaining ingredients. This can also be made vegan using quinoa and chickpeas for the protein and substituting with vegetable stock. I add ½ cup rinsed quinoa to the recipe and 1 can garbanzo beans (chickpeas).

Meatless

Slow-Cooker Tomato Soup

Becky Fixel, Grosse Pointe Farms, MI

Makes 8 servings

Prep. Time: 15 minutes · *Cooking Time: 6 hours* · *Ideal slow-cooker size: 6-qt.*

- 6–8 cups chopped fresh tomatoes
- 1 medium onion, chopped
- 2 tsp. minced garlic
- ½ tsp. pepper
- ½ tsp. sea salt
- ½ tsp. red pepper flakes
- 2 Tbsp. vegetable bouillon
- 1 cup water
- ¾ cup half-and-half
- 3 tsp. fresh chopped basil

1. Combine your tomatoes, onion, garlic, spices (minus the basil), bouillon, and 1 cup of water in your slow cooker.

2. Cover and cook on Low for 6 hours.

3. Add in your ¾ cup half-and-half and combine all ingredients with an immersion blender. Stir in the fresh basil, or garnish on top. Serve hot.

Cannellini Bean Soup

Hope Comerford, Clinton Township, MI

Makes 6–8 servings

Prep. Time: 10 minutes · *Soaking Time: overnight* · *Cooking Time: 30 minutes*

- 2 Tbsp. extra-virgin olive oil
- 4 cloves garlic, sliced very thin
- 1 small onion, chopped
- 2 heads escarole, well washed and cut medium-fine (about 8 cups)
- 8-oz. dry cannellini beans, soaked overnight
- 8 cups low-sodium vegetable stock
- 3 basil leaves, chopped fine
- Parmesan cheese shavings, *optional*

1. Set the Instant Pot to Sauté and heat the olive oil.
2. Sauté the garlic, onion, and escarole until the onion is translucent.
3. Hit the Cancel button on your Instant Pot and add the beans and vegetable stock.
4. Secure the lid and set the vent to sealing.
5. Manually set the time for 25 minutes on high pressure.
6. When the cooking time is over, let the pressure release naturally. Remove the lid when the pin drops and spoon into serving bowls.
7. Top each bowl with a sprinkle of the chopped basil leaves and a few Parmesan shavings (if using).

Tip:

If you do not remember to soak the beans overnight, or if you don't have time to soak them, simply cook the soup on high pressure for 51 minutes instead.

Minestrone

Bernita Boyts, Shawnee Mission, KS

Makes 8–10 servings

Prep. Time: 15 minutes ✤ *Cooking Time: 5–12 hours* ✤ *Ideal slow-cooker size: 3½- to 4-qt.*

1 large onion, chopped
4 carrots, sliced
3 stalks celery, sliced
2 cloves garlic, minced
1 Tbsp. olive oil
6 oz. tomato paste
2 cups chicken, beef, or vegetable broth
1 cup dried pinto beans, soaked overnight, rinsed
10-oz. pkg. frozen green beans
2–3 cups chopped cabbage
1 medium zucchini, sliced
8 cups water
2 Tbsp. parsley
2 Tbsp. Italian seasoning
1 tsp. sea salt, or more to taste
½ tsp. pepper
¾ cup dry acini di pepe (small round pasta)
Grated Parmesan or Asiago cheese, *optional*

1. Sauté onion, carrots, celery, and garlic in oil in skillet until tender. Add to slow cooker.
2. Combine all other ingredients, except pasta and cheese, in slow cooker.
3. Cover. Cook 5–6 hours on High or 10–12 hours on Low.
4. Add pasta 1 hour before cooking is complete.
5. Top individual servings with cheese, if desired.

Tip:

If you are short on time, or do not want to dirty more dishes, you do not need to sauté the onion, carrots, celery, and garlic in oil. Simply place those ingredients into the slow-cooker crock and continue on to step 2.

Black Bean Soup with Fresh Salsa

Hope Comerford, Clinton Township, MI

Makes 6–8 servings
Prep. Time: 5 minutes · *Cooking Time: 20 minutes*

1 cup dried black beans, soaked overnight, rinsed
7 cups chicken stock
5 cloves garlic, minced
1 Tbsp. chili powder
1½ tsp. cumin
1 tsp. salt
1 tsp. olive oil
3 Tbsp. sour cream, *optional*
3 tsp. chopped fresh oregano

Salsa:

⅓ cup fresh cilantro, washed and stemmed
½ onion, coarsely chopped
Juice of ½ lime
¼ tsp. salt

1. Place the beans, chicken stock, garlic, chili powder, cumin, salt, and olive oil into the inner pot of the Instant Pot.

2. Secure the lid and set the vent to sealing.

3. Manually set the cook time for 20 minutes on high pressure.

4. While the soup is cooking, puree the cilantro, onion, lime juice, and salt in a food processor until smooth. Place in a small bowl and keep refrigerated until serving time.

5. When the cooking time is over, let the pressure release naturally.

6. When the pin drops, remove the lid and scoop out about 1 cup of cooked beans with a slotted spoon and place in a bowl. Using an immersion blender, puree the beans then stir them back into the pot, along with the fresh oregano.

7. Spoon soup into serving bowls and serve with a bit of optional sour cream and fresh salsa on top.

Slow-Cooker Adaptation:

1. In a 6–7-qt. slow cooker, add the beans, chicken stock, garlic, chili powder, cumin, salt, and olive oil into the crock.

2. Cover and cook on Low for 10–12 hours, or on High for 5–6 hours.

3. When the cook time is up, remove the lid and scoop out about 1 cup of cooked beans with a slotted spoon and place in a bowl. Using an immersion blender, puree the beans, then stir them back into the crock, along with the fresh oregano.

4. Spoon soup into serving bowls and serve with a bit of optional sour cream and fresh salsa on top.

Sweet Potato Soup with Kale

Hope Comerford, Clinton Township, MI

Makes 8 servings
Prep. Time: 5 minutes ⁂ *Cooking Time: 5 minutes*

- 1 Tbsp. olive oil
- 1 medium onion, chopped
- 2 cloves garlic, chopped
- 2 lb. sweet potatoes, peeled and diced
- 5 cups chicken stock or vegetable stock
- 2 cups diced tomatoes
- 1 bay leaf
- 1 tsp. paprika
- ½ tsp. coriander
- 1 sprig fresh rosemary
- ¼ tsp. pepper
- 5 oz. chopped kale

1. Set the Instant Pot to Sauté and heat up the olive oil in the inner pot.
2. Sauté the onion and garlic in the heated oil for 3 to 5 minutes.
3. Press Cancel and add the sweet potatoes, stock, diced tomatoes, bay leaf, paprika, coriander, rosemary, and pepper to the inner pot.
4. Secure the lid and set the vent to sealing.
5. Manually set the Instant Pot to cook for 5 minutes on high pressure.
6. When the cooking time is over, let the pressure release naturally for 10 minutes, then manually release the rest of the pressure.
7. When the pin drops, remove the lid and gently stir the kale into the soup. Let the soup sit for a few minutes so the kale can wilt, then serve.

Slow-Cooker Adaptation:

1. In a 5–6-qt. slow cooker, combine all of the ingredients, except the kale.
2. Cover and cook on Low for 8–10 hours, or on High for 4–5 hours.
3. When cook time is over, remove the lid and stir in the kale and put the lid back on. Let the soup sit for a few minutes so the kale can wilt, then serve.

Potato Leek Soup

Melissa Paskvan, Novi, MI

Makes 4–6 servings

Prep. Time: 20 minutes · *Cooking Time: 6 hours* · *Ideal slow-cooker size: 6-qt.*

- 3 large leeks, chopped (rinse leek well and include the tough tops)
- 5 medium Yukon Gold potatoes, chopped
- 2 cups vegetable stock
- 2 cups water
- 2–3 bay leaves
- ½ head of cauliflower, broken up
- 3 stalks of celery, whole
- ¼ tsp pepper
- Salt to taste

1. Place all the ingredients except the salt in the slow cooker, and put the tough tops of the leeks on the top.

2. Cover and cook on Low for 6 hours.

3. Remove tough leek tops, celery, and bay leaves. Either blend all the ingredients in a blender or use an immersion blender while in the cooker and blend until very creamy. Salt to taste and add water if too thick for your liking.

Serving suggestion:

Serve with scallions on top for a vegan option, with Monterey Jack cheese and scallions for a vegetarian option, or with bacon bits, scallions, and cheese for a meat-eater option.

Creamy Potato Soup

Hope Comerford, Clinton Township, MI

Makes 6 servings

Prep. Time: 20 minutes · *Cooking Time: 8–10 hours* · *Ideal slow-cooker size: 5-qt.*

- 8–9 Idaho potatoes, chopped into bite-sized pieces
- 4½ cups vegetable stock
- ½ cup milk
- 1 medium onion, chopped
- 2–4 carrots, chopped
- 1–2 stalks celery, chopped
- 3 green onions, chopped
- 4 cloves garlic, minced
- 8-oz. block reduced-fat cream cheese, chopped into cubes
- ¼ cup nonfat plain Greek yogurt
- 3 Tbsp. cornstarch
- 2 Tbsp. butter
- 1 tsp. onion powder
- 1½ tsp. pepper
- 1 tsp. salt

1. Place all ingredients into your crock and stir.
2. Cook on Low for 8–10 hours.

Serving suggestion:

Serve with fresh chopped chives or green onions on top and little bit of shredded cheese.

Tip:

Use an immersion blender to give your soup a smoother and creamier texture.

SLOW COOKER

Creamy Butternut Squash Soup

Hope Comerford, Clinton Township, MI

Makes 4–6 servings

Prep. Time: 20 minutes · *Cooking Time: 8 hours* · *Ideal slow-cooker size: 3-qt.*

- 1½ lb. butternut squash, peeled and cut into 1-inch chunks
- 1 small onion, quartered
- 1 carrot, cut into 1-inch chunks
- 1 small sweet potato, cut into 1-inch chunks
- 2 tsp. freshly grated ginger
- ¼ tsp. cinnamon
- ⅛ tsp. nutmeg
- ½ tsp. sugar
- ¼ tsp. salt
- ⅛ tsp. pepper
- 3 cups vegetable stock (or you can use chicken stock)
- 1 cup half-and-half

1. Place the butternut squash, onion, carrot, sweet potato pieces, and ginger into your crock.

2. Sprinkle the contents of the crock with the cinnamon, nutmeg, sugar, salt, and pepper. Pour the stock over the top.

3. Cover and cook on Low for 8 hours, or until the vegetables are soft.

4. Using an immersion blender, blend the soup until smooth.

5. Remove ¼ cup of the soup and mix it with 1 cup of half-and-half. Pour this into the crock and mix until well combined.

Butternut Squash Soup with Thai Gremolata

Andy Wagner, Quarryville, PA

Makes 4–6 servings

Prep. Time: 25 minutes ✤ *Cooking Time: 2–5 hours* ✤ *Ideal slow-cooker size: 3½- or 4-qt.*

2 lb. butternut squash, peeled and cut into 1-inch pieces

2 cups vegetable broth

14-oz. can unsweetened coconut milk

¼ cup minced onions

1 Tbsp. brown sugar, packed

1 Tbsp. soy sauce or Bragg Liquid Aminos

½–1 tsp. crushed red pepper

2 Tbsp. fresh lime juice

Lime wedges, *optional*

Thai gremolata:

½ cup chopped fresh basil or cilantro

½ cup chopped peanuts

1 Tbsp. finely shredded lime peel

1. In a 3½- or 4-quart slow cooker, stir together squash, broth, coconut milk, onions, brown sugar, soy sauce, and crushed red pepper.

2. Cover and cook on Low for 4–5 hours or on High for 2–2½ hours.

3. Meanwhile, assemble the Thai Gremolata. Mix the basil, peanuts, and lime peel. Set aside.

4. Use an immersion or stand blender to carefully blend soup until completely smooth.

5. Stir in lime juice. Ladle into bowls and top with Thai Gremolata. If you wish, serve with lime wedges.

Main Dishes

Chicken & Turkey

Garlic and Lemon Chicken

Hope Comerford, Clinton Township, MI

Makes 5 servings

Prep. Time: 5 minutes · *Cooking Time: 5–6 hours* · *Ideal slow-cooker size: 3- or 5-qt.*

- 4–5 lb. boneless skinless chicken breasts or thighs
- ½ cup minced shallots
- 4 large cloves garlic, minced
- ½ cup olive oil
- ¼ cup lemon juice
- 1 Tbsp. no-salt seasoning
- ⅛ tsp. pepper

1. Place chicken in slow cooker.
2. In a small bowl, mix the remaining ingredients. Pour this mixture over the chicken in the crock.
3. Cover and cook on Low for 5–6 hours.

Serving suggestion:

Best Smashed Potatoes on page 178 and Garlic Butter Cauliflower on page 194 would make great sides for this dish.

Garlic Mushroom Thighs

Elaine Vigoda, Rochester, NY

Makes 6 servings

Prep. Time: 15 minutes · *Cooking Time: 7 hours* · *Ideal slow-cooker size: 5-qt.*

- 6 boneless skinless chicken thighs
- 3 Tbsp. all-purpose flour
- 8–10 cloves garlic, peeled and very lightly crushed
- 1 Tbsp. olive oil
- ¾ lb. fresh mushrooms, any combination of varieties, cut into bite-sized pieces
- ⅓ cup balsamic vinegar
- 1¼ cups chicken broth or stock
- 1–2 bay leaves
- ½ tsp. dried thyme or
- 4 sprigs fresh thyme
- 2 tsp. apricot preserves

Serving suggestion:

This would go well served with Thyme Roasted Sweet Potatoes on page 172.

1. Grease interior of slow cooker.
2. Place flour in a strong plastic bag without any holes. Once by one, put each thigh in bag, hold the bag shut, and shake it to flour the thigh fully.
3. Place thighs in the crock. If you need to make a second layer, stagger the pieces so they don't directly overlap.
4. If you have time, sauté the garlic in oil in skillet just until it begins to brown. Otherwise, use raw.
5. Sprinkle garlic over thighs, including those on bottom layer.
6. Scatter cut-up mushrooms over thighs too, remembering those on the bottom layer.
7. Mix remaining ingredients together in a bowl, stirring to break up the preserves.
8. When well mixed, pour into the cooker along the edges so you don't wash the vegetables off the chicken pieces.
9. Cover and cook on Low for 7 hours, or until an instant-read thermometer registers 160–165°F when stuck into the thighs.
10. Serve meat topped with vegetables with sauce spooned over.

Basil Chicken

Phyllis Good, Lancaster, PA

Makes 4–6 servings

Prep. Time: 15 minutes ஃ *Cooking Time: 4¼–4½ hours* ஃ *Ideal slow-cooker size: 4-qt.*

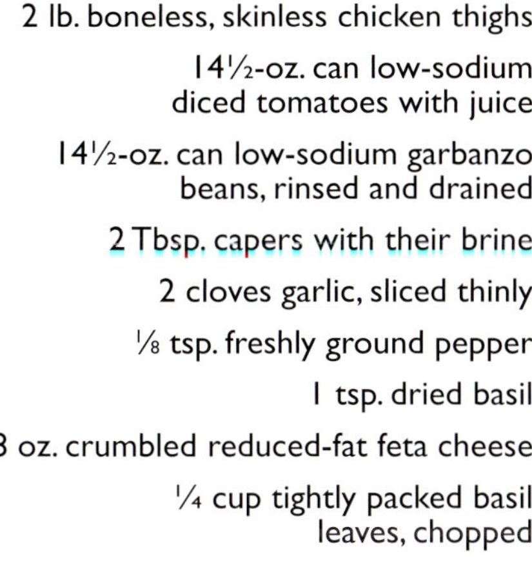

- 2 lb. boneless, skinless chicken thighs
- 14½-oz. can low-sodium diced tomatoes with juice
- 14½-oz. can low-sodium garbanzo beans, rinsed and drained
- 2 Tbsp. capers with their brine
- 2 cloves garlic, sliced thinly
- ⅛ tsp. freshly ground pepper
- 1 tsp. dried basil
- 8 oz. crumbled reduced-fat feta cheese
- ¼ cup tightly packed basil leaves, chopped

1. Place chicken in the slow cooker. Pour tomatoes, garbanzos, and capers on top.

2. Sprinkle with garlic slices, pepper, and dried basil.

3. Cover and cook on Low for 4 hours.

4. Sprinkle with feta. Cook on Low for 15 to 30 more minutes, or until chicken is done.

5. Sprinkle with fresh basil and serve.

Thyme and Garlic Turkey Breast

Hope Comerford, Clinton Township, MI

Makes 6–8 servings

Prep. Time: 10 minutes ❧ *Cooking Time: 7–8 hours* ❧ *Ideal slow-cooker size: 6- or 7-qt.*

4 lb. bone-in turkey breast, giblets removed, skin removed

¼ cup olive oil

1 Tbsp. balsamic vinegar

1 Tbsp. water

1 orange, juiced

6 cloves garlic, minced

1 Tbsp. fresh chopped thyme

1 tsp. onion powder

1 tsp. kosher salt

1. Place turkey breast in crock.

2. Mix together the remaining ingredients and pour over the turkey breast. Rub it in on all sides with clean hands.

3. Cover and cook on Low for 7–8 hours.

Serving suggestion:

This would go well served with Slow-Cooker Beets on page 182 and Thyme Roasted Sweet Potatoes on page 172.

Herbed Chicken

Phyllis Good, Lancaster, PA

Makes 4–6 servings

Prep. Time: 15 minutes · *Cooking Time: 4–6 hours* · *Ideal slow-cooker size: 6-qt.*

- 5-lb. roasting chicken
- 1 onion, quartered
- 2 cloves garlic, 1 sliced, 1 whole
- 1 Tbsp. fresh parsley, or 1 tsp. dried
- 1 Tbsp. fresh sage, or 1 tsp. dried
- 1 Tbsp. fresh rosemary, or 1 tsp. dried
- 1 Tbsp. fresh thyme, or 1 tsp. dried
- 1 Tbsp. butter, softened
- Paprika to taste
- Salt and pepper to taste

1. Grease crock of slow cooker. Clean and wash the chicken. Pat dry.
2. Put the quartered onion and sliced garlic into the bird's cavity. Stuff in the parsley, sage, rosemary, and thyme too.
3. Rub the outside of the chicken with the whole garlic clove, and then toss it into the cavity.
4. Rub the outside of the chicken with softened butter. Sprinkle with paprika, salt, and pepper.
5. Place chicken into the greased slow cooker.
6. Cover. Cook on Low 4–6 hours, or until the meat is tender, the drumsticks move freely, and the juices run clear.
7. Lift the chicken out of the cooker onto a platter. Cover with foil to keep warm. Let it stand for 15 minutes before cutting it up.
8. Thicken the chicken stock to make gravy. Or use the broth to make rice.

Serving suggestions:

This would go well served with Steamed Veggie Medley on page 193 and Quinoa with Spinach on page 150.

Chicken Dinner in a Packet

Bonnie Whaling, Clearfield, PA

Makes 4 servings
Prep. Time: 10 minutes ❧ *Cooking Time: 15 minutes*

- 1 cup water
- 4 (5-oz.) boneless, skinless chicken breast halves
- 2 cups sliced fresh mushrooms
- 2 medium carrots, cut in thin strips, about 1 cup
- 1 medium zucchini, unpeeled and sliced, about 1½ cups
- 2 Tbsp. olive oil or canola oil
- 2 Tbsp. lemon juice
- 1 tsp. fresh basil or 1 tsp. dry basil
- ¼ tsp. salt
- ¼ tsp. black pepper

1. Pour the water into the inner pot of the Instant Pot and place the trivet or a steamer basket on top.
2. Fold four 12 × 28-inch pieces of foil in half to make four 12 × 14-inch rectangles. Place one chicken breast half on each piece of foil.
3. Top with the mushrooms, carrots, and zucchini, dividing the vegetables equally between the chicken bundles.
4. In a small bowl, stir together the oil, lemon juice, basil, salt, and pepper.
5. Drizzle the oil mixture over the vegetables and chicken.
6. Pull up two opposite edges of foil. Seal with a double fold. Then fold in the remaining edges, leaving enough space for steam to build.
7. Place the bundles on top of the trivet, or inside the steamer basket.
8. Secure the lid and set the vent to sealing.
9. Manually set the cook time for 15 minutes at high pressure.
10. When the cooking time is over, let the pressure release naturally. When the pin drops, remove the lid.
11. Serve dinners in foil packets, or transfer to serving plate.

Tuscan Chicken

Hope Comerford, Clinton Township, MI

Makes 4 servings

Prep. Time: 5 minutes *Cooking Time: 10 minutes*

2 lb. boneless, skinless chicken thighs
½ tsp. salt
½ tsp. onion powder
½ tsp. Italian seasoning
¼ tsp. pepper
3 Tbsp. butter
6 cloves garlic, minced
¾ cup sliced baby bella mushrooms
¾ cup chicken stock
½ tsp. red pepper flakes
1 cup heavy cream
2 cups spinach
½ cup sliced sun-dried tomatoes
½ cup shredded Asiago cheese

1. Coat the chicken with the salt, onion powder, Italian seasoning, and pepper.

2. Set the Instant Pot to the Sauté function and let it get hot. Add the butter to melt.

3. When the butter is melted, immediately add the chicken to the inner pot to sear.

4. Once the chicken is seared on both sides, add the garlic and mushrooms. Sauté for about 1 minute.

5. Pour in the chicken stock and carefully deglaze the bottom of the pot, scraping up any stuck-on bits. Press Cancel.

6. Sprinkle in the red pepper flakes, then secure the lid and set the vent to sealing.

7. Manually set the cook time for 5 minutes on high pressure.

8. When cook time is up, manually release the pressure.

9. When the pin drops, remove the lid. Press Cancel, then Sauté. Remove the chicken and set aside.

10. Stir in the heavy cream slowly, then add the spinach, sun-dried tomatoes, and cheese. Once mixed, serve the chicken with the sauce over the top.

Chicken Casablanca

Joyce Kaut, Rochester, NY

Makes 8 servings

Prep. Time: 20 minutes *Cooking Time: 12 minutes*

- 2 Tbsp. canola oil, *divided*
- 2 large onions, sliced
- ¼ cup freshly grated ginger
- 3 cloves garlic, minced
- 3 lb. boneless, skinless chicken breasts, cut into bite-sized pieces
- 3 large carrots, diced
- ½ tsp. ground cumin
- ½ tsp. salt
- ½ tsp. pepper
- ¼ tsp. cinnamon
- 2 Tbsp. raisins
- 14½-oz. can reduced-sodium diced tomatoes
- 3 small zucchini, sliced
- 15-oz. can garbanzo beans, drained, rinsed
- 2 Tbsp. chopped fresh parsley

1. Using the Sauté function of the Instant Pot, heat 1 Tbsp. of the oil. Cook the onions, ginger, and garlic for 5 minutes, stirring constantly. Remove the onions, ginger, and garlic from the pot and set aside.

2. Brown the chicken pieces with the remaining oil, then add the cooked onions, ginger, and garlic back in as well as all the remaining ingredients, except the parsley. Press Cancel.

3. Secure the lid and make sure vent is in the sealing position. Cook on Manual mode for 12 minutes.

4. When the cooking time is over, let the pressure release naturally for 5 minutes and then release the rest of the pressure manually.

5. Garnish with the parsley.

Juicy Orange Chicken

Andrea Maher, Dunedin, FL

Makes 6 servings

Prep. Time: 10 minutes ✿ *Cooking Time: 3–8 hours* ✿ *Ideal slow-cooker size: 5- or 6-qt.*

18–24 oz. boneless, skinless chicken breast, cut into small pieces

1 cup freshly squeezed orange juice

¼ cup honey

6 small oranges, peeled and sliced

¼ cup Bragg Liquid Aminos

6 cups broccoli slaw

1. Add all the ingredients to the slow cooker except the broccoli slaw.
2. Cover and cook on High 3–4 hours or Low 6–8 hours.
3. Divide mixture between 6 mason jars.
4. Add 1 cup broccoli slaw to each mason jar.
5. Pour into a bowl when you're ready to eat!

Lime-Like Key West Chicken

Maria Shevlin, Sicklerville, NJ

Makes 4 servings

Prep. Time: 5 minutes · *Cooking Time: 12 minutes*

1 Tbsp. avocado oil
2 cloves garlic, minced
2½ lb. boneless skinless chicken breasts
½ tsp. garlic powder
½ tsp salt
¼ tsp white pepper
1 Tbsp. parsley flakes
¼ cup chicken stock
¼ cup coconut aminos or tamari
Juice and zest of 1 lime
2 Tbsp. honey
2 Tbsp. brown sugar

1. Set the Instant Pot to the Sauté function. Add the avocado oil and minced garlic to the inner pot and sauté for 2 minutes. Press Cancel.
2. Add the chicken, garlic powder, salt, white pepper, and parsley flakes to the inner pot. Mix well to coat.
3. In a small bowl, combine the chicken stock, coconut aminos, lime juice, zest, honey, and brown sugar.
4. Pour over the chicken.
5. Secure the lid and set the vent to sealing.
6. Manually set the cook time for 12 minutes on high pressure.
7. When cook time is up, let the pressure release naturally for 10 minutes, then manually release any remaining pressure.

Serving suggestion:
Serve as tacos if using shredded.

Optional:
Remove and shred the chicken with a hand mixer, then return it back to the pot and stir it into the juices.

Italian Chicken Wraps

Hope Comerford, Clinton Township, MI

Makes 4–6 servings

Prep. Time: 20 minutes · *Cooking Time: 4 hours*

Marinating Time: 4–8 hours or overnight · *Ideal slow-cooker size: 3-qt.*

- 1 lb. boneless, skinless chicken breasts
- ¾ cup olive oil
- 3 Tbsp. white wine vinegar
- 3 Tbsp. freshly squeezed lemon juice
- 1½ tsp. honey
- ¾ tsp. Dijon mustard
- 2 cloves garlic, minced
- ¼ cup freshly chopped parsley
- 3 tsp. freshly chopped oregano
- 2 tsp. freshly chopped basil
- 1 tsp. freshly chopped thyme
- ½ tsp. salt
- ¼ tsp. freshly ground pepper
- 1 green bell pepper, sliced in ribs
- 1 red bell pepper, sliced in ribs
- 1 medium onion, sliced in rings
- 10 (10-inch) flour or corn tortillas

Optional toppings (choose all or some):

- Freshly grated Parmesan cheese
- Pepperoncini rings
- Shredded lettuce
- Chopped tomatoes
- Chopped fresh basil

1. Cut chicken into thin strips.

2. In a large mixing bowl, combine the olive oil, white wine vinegar, lemon juice, honey, Dijon mustard, garlic, herbs, salt, and pepper. Mix well. Add the chicken and coat evenly. Cover the bowl and marinate 4–8 hours or overnight in the fridge.

3. Pour chicken and marinade into slow cooker along with the peppers. Cook on Low for 4 hours, until chicken is white through the middle and tender.

4. Serve with tortillas and desired optional toppings.

Chicken Rice Bake

Nanci Keatley, Salem, OR

Makes 6 servings

Prep. Time: 8 minutes · *Cooking Time: 22 minutes* · *Standing Time: 10 minutes*

- 1 Tbsp. olive oil
- 1 cup finely diced onions
- 1 tsp. chopped fresh garlic
- 1 cup chopped celery
- 2 lb. boneless, skinless chicken breasts, cut into bite-sized pieces
- 1 cup chopped carrots
- 2 cups sliced fresh mushrooms
- 1½ cups uncooked brown rice
- 1½ tsp. salt
- 1 tsp. pepper
- 1 tsp. dill weed
- 1½ cups low-sodium chicken broth

1. Set the Instant Pot to the Sauté function and heat the oil in the inner pot.
2. Sauté the onions and garlic for 3 minutes. Add the celery and sauté an additional 3 minutes.
3. Press Cancel. Add the chicken and spread out evenly, Add the carrots and mushrooms and spread out evenly.
4. Pour the rice evenly on top and sprinkle with the seasonings. Last, pour in the chicken broth. Do not stir.
5. Set the cook time manually to cook for 22 minutes on high pressure.
6. When the cooking time is over, manually release the pressure.
7. Allow to stand 10 minutes before serving.

Crustless Chicken Pot Pie

Hope Comerford, Clinton Township, MI

Makes 6 servings

Prep. Time: 15 minutes · *Cooking Time: 30 minutes*

- 1 lb. boneless, skinless chicken breasts
- 3 Yukon Gold potatoes, peeled and chopped into ½-inch cubes
- 1 cup chopped onion
- 2 carrots, chopped
- ¾ cup frozen peas
- ¾ cup frozen corn
- ½ cup chopped celery
- 1 cup milk
- 1 cup chicken broth
- 1 tsp. salt
- 1 tsp. garlic powder
- 1 tsp. onion powder
- 2 Tbsp. cornstarch
- 2 Tbsp. cold water
- 16.3-oz. can flaky biscuits

1. Place all the ingredients, except for the cornstarch, water, and biscuits, into the inner pot of the Instant Pot.

2. Secure the lid and set the vent to sealing. Manually set the cook time for 25 minutes on high pressure.

3. While the Instant Pot is cooking, bake the canned biscuits according to the directions on the can.

4. When the cook time is over, manually release the pressure.

5. When the pin drops, remove the lid. Remove the chicken to a bowl. Press Cancel then press Sauté.

6. Mix together the cornstarch and water. Stir this into the contents of the Instant Pot and cook until thickened, about 5 minutes. Meanwhile, shred the chicken, then add it back in with the contents of the inner pot.

7. Serve with the freshly baked flaky biscuits.

Insta Pasta à la Maria

Maria Shevlin, Sicklerville, MI

Makes 6–8 servings
Prep. Time: 10–15 minutes · *Cooking Time: 6 minutes*

- 4 cups homemade pasta sauce (see page 158 for a recipe)
- 2 cups fresh chopped spinach
- 1 cup chopped mushrooms
- ½ precooked chicken, shredded
- 1 tsp. salt
- ½ tsp. black pepper
- ½ tsp. dried basil
- ¼ tsp. red pepper flakes
- 13¼-oz. box pasta, any shape or brand
- 3 cups water
- ¼ cup freshly chopped parsley

1. Place the sauce in the bottom of the inner pot of the Instant Pot.
2. Add in the spinach, then the mushrooms.
3. Add the chicken on top of the veggies and sauce.
4. Add the seasonings and give it a stir to mix.
5. Add the box of pasta.
6. Add 3 cups of water.
7. Secure the lid and move vent to sealing. Manually set for 6 minutes on high pressure.
8. When cook time is up, release the pressure manually.
9. Remove the lid and stir in parsley.

Zucchini Vegetable Pot

Edwina Stoltzfus, Narvon, PA

Makes 6 servings

Prep. Time: 40 minutes · *Cooking Time: 3–4 hours* · *Ideal slow-cooker size: 3½- or 4-qt.*

- 1 lb. lean ground turkey
- 2 cups diced zucchini
- 2 ribs celery, chopped
- ¼ cup chopped green bell peppers
- 1 large onion, chopped
- 2 large tomatoes, chopped
- 1 clove garlic, chopped
- ¼ cup brown rice, uncooked
- ¾ tsp. sea salt
- ⅛ tsp. nutmeg
- ¼ tsp. black pepper
- 1 tsp. gluten-free Worcestershire sauce

1. Brown turkey in nonstick skillet.
2. Meanwhile, place zucchini, celery, bell peppers, onion, tomatoes, and garlic in slow cooker. Top with rice and ground turkey.
3. Sprinkle seasonings over top and add Worcestershire sauce.
4. Cover and cook on High for 3–4 hours.

Jazzed-Up Barbecue Pulled Chicken

Hope Comerford, Clinton Township, MI

Makes 6–8 servings

Prep. Time: 5 minutes ⁂ *Cooking Time: 6–7 hours* ⁂ *Ideal slow-cooker size: 4-qt.*

- 2 lb. boneless skinless chicken breasts
- 1 cup ketchup
- ¼ cup molasses
- 2 Tbsp. apple cider vinegar
- 2 Tbsp. Worcestershire sauce
- 1 clove garlic, minced
- 2 tsp. dry mustard
- 2 Tbsp. freshly squeezed orange juice
- 1 tsp. orange zest

1. Place chicken in crock.
2. In a bowl, mix the ketchup, molasses, apple cider vinegar, Worcestershire sauce, minced garlic, dry mustard, orange juice, and orange zest. Pour over the chicken.
3. Cover and cook on Low for 6–7 hours.
4. Remove the chicken and shred between two forks, then stir back through the sauce in the crock.

Serving suggestions:

- Serve on buns with your favorite toppings.
- This would be great served alongside Aunt Twila's Beans on page 174 and Chili-Lime Corn on the Cob on page 183.

Pork

Pork Roast and Vegetables

Jenny R. Unternahrer, Wayland, IA

Makes 8–10 servings

Prep. Time: 15 minutes ⁂ *Cooking Time: 6–8 hours* ⁂ *Ideal slow-cooker size: 5-qt.*

- 3 Tbsp. olive oil
- 3–4-lb. boneless pork chuck roast, trimmed
- Salt and pepper to taste
- ¼ cup all-purpose flour
- 2 Tbsp. tomato paste
- ½ cup dry white wine
- 1½ cups beef or chicken broth
- 1 Tbsp. Worcestershire sauce
- 1 medium onion, thinly sliced
- Handful baby carrots
- 2 small stalks celery, thinly sliced
- 3 cloves garlic, diced
- ½ tsp. dried thyme
- 1 lb. small potatoes, quartered

1. Heat oil in pan (preferably not a nonstick). Sprinkle roast with salt and pepper. Sear roast on all sides until browned, approximately 10 minutes. Place in large slow cooker.

2. Add flour and tomato paste to pan and cook for 1 minute. Add wine, broth, and Worcestershire sauce, scraping the bits off the bottom of the pan.

3. Pour over roast. Mix vegetables, garlic, and dried thyme in bowl and add to crock.

4. Cover and cook for 6–8 hours on Low. Add quartered potatoes to liquid after 4 hours. Serve in bowl so you can ladle the gravy over the top.

Pork and Sweet Potatoes

Vera F. Schmucker, Goshen, IN

Makes 4 servings

Prep. Time: 15 minutes ♧ *Cooking Time: 4–4½ hours* ♧ *Ideal slow-cooker size: 4-qt.*

4 pork loin chops

Salt and pepper, to taste

4 sweet potatoes, peeled and cut into large chunks

2 onions, cut in quarters

½ cup apple cider

1. Place meat in bottom of slow cooker. Salt and pepper to taste.

2. Arrange sweet potatoes and onions over the pork, then pour the apple cider over the top.

3. Cover and cook on High for 30 minutes and then on Low for 3½ to 4 hours, or until meat and vegetables are tender but not dry.

Serving suggestion:

This would be great served with Rosemary Carrots on page 185.

Carnitas

Hope Comerford, Clinton Township, MI

Makes 12 servings

Prep. Time: 10 minutes *Cooking Time: 15 minutes*

2 lb. pork shoulder roast, cut into 1-inch chunks

1½ tsp. kosher salt

½ tsp. pepper

2 tsp. cumin

5 cloves garlic, minced

3 tsp. fresh chopped oregano

3 bay leaves

2 cups chicken stock

1 tsp. lime zest

2 Tbsp. fresh lime juice

12 (6-inch) white corn tortillas, warmed

1. Place all ingredients, except the lime zest, lime juice, and tortillas, into the inner pot of the Instant Pot.
2. Secure the lid and set the vent to sealing. Manually set the cook time for 15 minutes on high pressure.
3. When cook time is up, let the pressure release naturally. When the pin drops, remove the lid. Remove the bay leaves and discard.
4. Remove the pork and shred it between 2 forks. Place it back in the pot along with the lime juice and lime zest. Stir.
5. Serve on the white corn tortillas.

Slow-Cooker Adaptation:

1. In a 4-quart slow cooker, place the pork shoulder roast WHOLE in the crock.
2. Mix the salt, pepper, cumin, garlic, and oregano. Rub it onto the pork roast.
3. Place the bay leaves around the pork roast, then pour in the chicken stock around the roast, being careful not to wash off the spices.
4. Cover and cook on low for 10–12 hours.
5. Remove the bay leaves and discard.
6. Remove the roast with a slotted spoon. Shred the pork between 2 forks, then replace the shredded pork in the crock along with the lime juice and lime zest. Stir.
7. Serve on warmed white corn tortillas.

Serving suggestion:

These would be great served with Cilantro Lime Rice on page 171.

Pork Chops with Potatoes and Green Beans

Hope Comerford, Clinton Township, MI

Makes 4 servings

Prep. Time: 8 minutes · *Cooking Time: 13 minutes*

- 2 Tbsp. olive oil, *divided*
- 4 boneless pork chops, 1–1½ inches thick
- Salt and pepper to taste
- 1 cup chicken broth
- 2 lb. baby potatoes, sliced in half
- 1 lb. fresh green beans, ends trimmed
- 3 cloves garlic, crushed
- 2 tsp. salt
- 1 tsp. onion powder
- 3 tsp. fresh chopped rosemary
- 1½ tsp. fresh chopped thyme
- ¼ tsp. pepper

1. Set the Instant Pot to Sauté and let it get hot. Add 1 Tbsp. of the oil.
2. Sprinkle each side of the pork chops with salt and pepper. Brown them on each side in the Instant Pot. Remove them when done.
3. Pour in the broth and scrape the bottom of the pot, bringing up any stuck-on bits. Press Cancel.
4. Arrange the pork chops back in the inner pot of the Instant Pot.
5. In a medium bowl, toss the potatoes and green beans with the garlic, salt, onion powder, rosemary, thyme, and pepper. Pour them over the pork chops.
6. Secure the lid and set the vent to sealing. Manually set the cook time for 8 minutes on high pressure.
7. When cook time is up, let the pressure release naturally for 10 minutes, then manually release the remaining pressure.

Tender and Tangy Ribs

Betty Moore, Plano, IL
Renee Shirk, Mount Joy, PA

Makes 2–3 servings

Prep. Time: 10 minutes ❀ *Cooking Time: 4–6 hours* ❀ *Ideal slow-cooker size: 2- to 3-qt.*

¾–1 cup vinegar
½ cup ketchup
2 Tbsp. sugar
2 Tbsp. Worcestershire sauce
1 clove garlic, minced
1 tsp. dry mustard
1 tsp. paprika
½ tsp. salt
⅛ tsp. pepper
2 lb. pork spareribs
1 Tbsp. oil

1. Combine all ingredients except spareribs and oil in slow cooker.

2. Brown ribs in oil in skillet. Transfer to slow cooker.

3. Cover. Cook on Low 4–6 hours.

Serving suggestion:

These would be great served with Aunt Twila's Beans on page 174 and Chili-Lime Corn on the Cob on page 183.

Kielbasa and Cabbage

Mary Ann Lefever, Lancaster, PA

Makes 4 servings

Prep. Time: 10–15 minutes · *Cooking Time: 8 hours* · *Ideal slow-cooker size: 4- or 5-qt.*

- 1 lb. kielbasa, cut into 4 chunks
- 4 large white potatoes, cut into chunks
- 1 Tbsp. salt, *divided*
- ¼ tsp. pepper, *divided*
- 1-lb. head green cabbage, shredded
- 4–5 large tomatoes, chopped
- 1 small onion, thinly sliced, *optional*

1. Layer the kielbasa then the potatoes into the slow cooker, and season with a bit of the salt and pepper. Add the cabbage.

2. Pour tomatoes over the top and sprinkle with the remaining salt and pepper.

3. Top with sliced onion if you wish.

4. Cover. Cook on Low 8 hours, or until meat is cooked through and vegetables are as tender as you like them.

Tip:

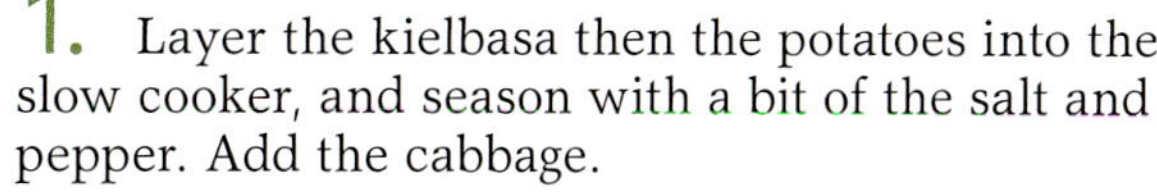

Sausage, Carrots, Potatoes, and Green Beans

Hope Comerford, Clinton Township, MI

Makes 4 servings

Prep. Time: 5 minutes ❧ *Cooking Time: 10 minutes*

1 Tbsp. olive oil
4 Tbsp. butter
1 large onion, sliced
14-oz. pkg. smoked sausage, sliced
1 cup chicken broth
2 carrots, peeled and chopped
2 lb. red potatoes, chopped
½ lb. fresh green beans, chopped
1½ tsp. sea salt
1½ tsp. smoked paprika
1 tsp. onion powder
¼ tsp. pepper

1. Set the Instant Pot to the Sauté function and let it get hot. Pour in the oil and butter.

2. Sauté the onion and sausage for about 4 minutes.

3. Pour in the broth and deglaze the bottom of the inner pot, scraping up any stuck-on bits with a wooden spoon. Press Cancel.

4. Add the remaining ingredients in the order listed.

5. Secure the lid and set the vent to sealing. Manually set the cook time for 6 minutes on high pressure.

6. When cook time is up, manually release the pressure.

Beef

Pot Roast

Carole Whaling, New Tripoli, PA

Makes 8 servings

Prep. Time: 20 minutes ❧ *Cooking Time: 35 minutes*

2 Tbsp. olive oil

3–4-lb. rump roast, or pot roast, bone removed, and cut into serving-sized pieces, trimmed of fat

4 medium potatoes, cubed or sliced

4 medium carrots, sliced

1 medium onion, sliced

4 cloves garlic, crushed

1 tsp. salt

½ tsp. pepper

1 cup beef broth

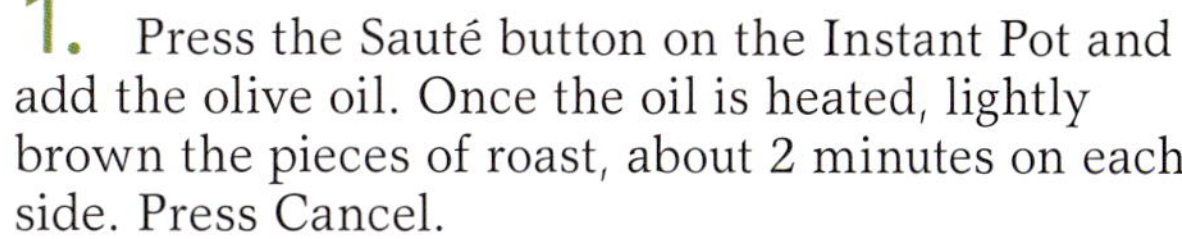

1. Press the Sauté button on the Instant Pot and add the olive oil. Once the oil is heated, lightly brown the pieces of roast, about 2 minutes on each side. Press Cancel.

2. Leave roast in Instant Pot and add the veggies and garlic around the roast, along with the salt, pepper, and beef broth.

3. Secure the lid and make sure the vent is set to sealing. Set the Instant Pot to Manual mode for 35 minutes. Let pressure release naturally when cook time is up.

Slow-Cooker Adaptation:

1. Place the roast WHOLE into a 5-qt slow cooker. Add the veggies and garlic around the roast, along with the salt, pepper, and beef broth.

2. Cover and cook on Low for 8–10 hours, or High for 4–5 hours.

Carolina Pot Roast

Jonathan Gehman, Harrisonburg, VA

Makes 3–4 servings

Prep. Time: 20 minutes · *Cooking Time: 3 hours* · *Ideal slow-cooker size: 3-qt.*

- 3 medium-large sweet potatoes, peeled and cut into 1-inch chunks
- ½ cup brown sugar
- 1-lb. chuck roast
- Scant ¼ tsp. cumin
- Salt to taste

1. Place sweet potatoes in bottom of slow cooker. Sprinkle brown sugar over potatoes.
2. Heat nonstick skillet over medium-high heat. Add roast and brown on all sides. Sprinkle meat with cumin and salt while browning. Place roast on top of potatoes.
3. Add an inch of water to the cooker, being careful not to wash the seasoning off the meat.
4. Cover and cook on Low 3 hours, or until meat and potatoes are tender but not dry or mushy.

Serving suggestion:

This would be great served with Orange-Glazed Carrots on page 186.

Red Wine Apple Roast

Rose Hankins, Stevensville, MD

Makes 10 servings

Prep. Time: 15 minutes · *Cooking Time: 6–8 hours* · *Ideal slow-cooker size: 4- or 5-qt.*

- 3-lb. eye of round beef roast
- 3 cups thinly sliced onions
- 1½ cups chopped apples, peeled or unpeeled
- 3 cloves garlic, chopped
- 1 cup red wine
- Salt and pepper to taste

1. Put roast in slow cooker. Layer onions, apples, and garlic on top of roast.

2. Carefully pour wine over roast without disturbing its toppings.

3. Sprinkle with salt and pepper to taste.

4. Cover. Cook on Low for 6 to 8 hours, or until meat is tender but not dry.

Serving suggestion:

This would be great served with Wild Mushrooms Italian on page 196.

Braised Beef with Cranberries

Audrey L. Kneer, Williamsfield, IL

Makes 8 servings
Prep. Time: 20 minutes · *Cooking Time: 60 minutes*

2 lb. sliced, well-trimmed top round beef
⅛ tsp. pepper
1 Tbsp. olive oil
1 medium onion, chopped
2 cloves garlic, chopped
½ cup peeled and diced turnip
1 medium carrot, chopped
1 celery rib, cut fine
1 cup apple juice
1 cup fresh or frozen cranberries
1 sprig fresh parsley
1 bay leaf

1. Rub the beef with pepper. Set aside.

2. Set the Instant Pot to Sauté and heat the olive oil in the inner pot.

3. Sauté the beef for about 10 minutes, searing each side.

4. Remove the beef and set it aside.

5. Sauté the onion and garlic for about 3 minutes, then add the turnip, carrot, and celery and continue sautéing for about 5 more minutes.

6. Pour in the apple juice and scrape the bottom of the pot to deglaze.

7. Press Cancel. Add the beef back in, and add the cranberries, parsley, and bay leaf. Make sure the sprig of parsley and bay leaf are tucked into the liquid.

8. Secure the lid and set the vent to sealing.

9. Set the cook time manually for 60 minutes on high pressure.

10. When the cooking time is over, let the pressure release naturally for 10 minutes, then manually release the remaining pressure.

Slow-Cooker Adaptation

1. Rub the beef with the pepper, then place the beef WHOLE into a 5-qt slow cooker.

2. Place the remaining ingredients into the slow cooker, making sure the sprig of parsley and bay leaf are tucked into the liquid.

3. Cover and cook on Low for 10–12 hours, or High for 5–6 hours.

Instant
Soup
Meat

Espresso Braised Beef

Dena Mell-Dorchy, Royal Oak, MI

Makes 6 servings

Prep. Time: 25 minutes · *Cooking Time: 8–9 hours* · *Ideal slow-cooker size: 3- or 4-qt.*

1 large onion, cut into wedges
3 medium carrots, cut into ½-inch pieces
1 medium turnip, cut into 1-inch pieces
3 celery stalks, cut into 1-inch pieces
1½ lb. boneless beef chuck, cut into 1-inch pieces
⅔ cup beef stock
2 Tbsp. tomato paste
1 Tbsp. instant espresso coffee powder
1 tsp. packed brown sugar
3 tsp. fresh chopped thyme
3 tsp. fresh chopped rosemary
½ tsp. sea salt
¼ tsp. pepper

1. Spray slow cooker with nonstick cooking spray.
2. In crock, combine onion, carrots, turnip, and celery. Top with beef.
3. Whisk together stock, tomato paste, espresso coffee powder, brown sugar, thyme, rosemary, salt, and pepper. Pour over beef and vegetables in crock.
4. Cover and cook on Low for 8–9 hours.

Serving suggestion:
Serve over cooked brown rice or quinoa.

Hungarian Beef with Paprika

Maureen Csikasz, Wakefield, MA

Makes 9 servings

Prep. Time: 15 minutes ❧ *Cooking Time: 3–6 hours* ❧ *Ideal slow-cooker size: oval 5- or 6-qt.*

- 3 lb. boneless chuck roast
- 2–3 medium onions, coarsely chopped
- 5 Tbsp. sweet paprika
- ¾ tsp. salt
- ¼ tsp. black pepper
- ½ tsp. caraway seeds
- 1 clove garlic, chopped
- ½ green bell pepper, sliced
- ¼ cup water
- ½ cup nonfat plain Greek yogurt
- Fresh parsley

Serving suggestion:
This would be great served alongside Broccoli and Bell Peppers on page 191.

1. Grease interior of slow-cooker crock.
2. Place roast in crock.
3. In a good-sized bowl, mix all ingredients together, except nonfat plain Greek yogurt and parsley.
4. Spoon mixture evenly over roast.
5. Cover. Cook on High 3–4 hours, or on Low 5–6 hours, or until instant-read meat thermometer registers 140–145°F when stuck in center of meat.
6. When finished cooking, use sturdy tongs or 2 metal spatulas to lift meat to cutting board. Cover with foil to keep warm. Let stand 10–15 minutes.
7. Cut into chunks or slices.
8. Just before serving, dollop with nonfat plain Greek yogurt. Garnish with fresh parsley.

Korean Beef

Hope Comerford, Clinton Township, MI

Makes 8–10 servings
Prep. Time: 8–10 minutes · *Cooking Time: 70 minutes*

1 medium onion
1 McIntosh apple, peeled, cored
5 cloves garlic
¼ cup rice vinegar
1 tsp. hot sauce
2 Tbsp. low-sodium soy sauce
¼ cup fresh grated ginger
1 Tbsp. chili powder
¼ tsp. red pepper flakes
3 Tbsp. brown sugar
1 cup ketchup
2–3-lb. chuck roast
1 cup beef broth

1. In a food processor, puree the onion, apple, and garlic. Pour this mixture into a bowl and mix it with the rice vinegar, hot sauce, soy sauce, ginger, chili powder, red pepper flakes, brown sugar, and ketchup.

2. Place the pork roast into the bottom of the inner pot of the Instant Pot. Pour the sauce over the top and turn it so it's covered on all sides. Add the beef broth.

3. Secure the lid and set the vent to sealing. Manually set the cook time for 70 minutes on high pressure.

4. When cook time is up, let the pressure release naturally, then remove lid when the pin drops.

5. Remove the chuck roast and shred it between 2 forks. Return the shredded pork to the inner pot and mix it through the sauce.

Serving suggestion:

Serve over brown rice or quinoa with a side of bok choi sautéed in toasted sesame seed oil and red pepper flakes.

Beef with Broccoli

Genelle Taylor, Perrysburg, OH

Makes 4 servings

Prep. Time: 10 minutes *Cooking Time: 5–6 hours* *Ideal slow-cooker size: 5- or 6-qt.*

- 1 cup beef broth
- ½ cup low-sodium soy sauce
- ⅓ cup brown sugar
- 1 Tbsp. sesame oil
- 3 cloves garlic, minced
- 1½ lb. boneless beef chuck roast or steak, sliced into thin strips
- 2 Tbsp. cornstarch
- 14-oz fresh broccoli florets

1. In a mixing bowl, whisk together the beef broth, soy sauce, brown sugar, sesame oil, and garlic.
2. Lay the beef strips in slow cooker and pour the sauce over, tossing the strips to coat.
3. Cover and cook on Low for 5 to 6 hours
4. Remove 4 Tbsp. of the sauce and whisk it in a small bowl with cornstarch. Slowly stir this into slow cooker.
5. Add broccoli. Cook an additional 30 minutes.

Cuban Steak for Salad

Hope Comerford, Clinton Township, MI

Makes 6–8 servings

Prep. Time: 10 minutes ✿ *Marinating Time: 2–8 hours*
Cooking Time: 6 hours ✿ *Ideal slow-cooker size: 3-qt.*

2 lb. skirt steak
2 limes, juiced
1 orange, juiced
¼ cup olive oil
3 cloves garlic, minced
1 tsp. kosher salt
¼ tsp. pepper
¼ tsp. cumin
Salad greens
Salad dressing of choice

1. Place skirt steak in a ziplock bag.
2. In a small bowl, mix the remaining ingredients, except the salad greens and dressing. Pour this over the steak in the bag, seal it, and refrigerate it for 2–8 hours.
3. Place the skirt steak with marinade in the crock.
4. Cover and cook on Low for 6 hours.
5. Remove the steak and let it rest on a cutting board for about 5 minutes. Slice into thin strips against the grain.
6. Serve over salad greens with a light dressing.

Four-Pepper Steak

Renee Hankins, Narvon, PA

Makes 14 servings

Prep. Time: 30 minutes ❧ *Cooking Time: 5–8 hours* ❧ *Ideal slow-cooker size: 4- or 5-qt.*

1 yellow pepper, sliced into ¼-inch thick pieces

1 red pepper, sliced into ¼-inch thick pieces

1 orange pepper, sliced into ¼-inch thick pieces

1 green pepper, sliced into ¼-inch thick pieces

2 cloves garlic, sliced

2 large onions, sliced

1 tsp. ground cumin

1½ tsp. fresh chopped oregano

1 bay leaf

3 lb. flank steak, cut in ¼–½-inch-thick slices across the grain

Salt to taste

3½ cups diced tomatoes

Sliced jalapeño peppers, *optional*

1. Place sliced bell peppers, garlic, onions, cumin, oregano, and bay leaf in slow cooker. Stir gently to mix.

2. Put steak slices on top of vegetable mixture. Season with salt.

3. Spoon tomatoes with any juice over top. Sprinkle with jalapeño pepper slices if you wish. Do not stir.

4. Cover and cook on Low 5–8 hours, depending on your slow cooker. Check after 5 hours to see if meat is tender. If not, continue cooking until tender but not dry. Remove bay leaf and serve.

Serving suggestion:

This would be great served alongside Veggie Loaded Rice on page 170.

Slow-Cooker Swiss Steak

Joyce Bowman, Lady Lake, FL

Makes 4 servings

Prep. Time: 10 minutes · *Cooking Time: 7 hours* · *Ideal slow-cooker size: 3-qt.*

- 1-lb. round steak, ¾–1-inch thick, cubed
- 16-oz. stewed tomatoes
- 3 carrots, halved lengthwise
- 2 potatoes, quartered
- 1 medium onion, quartered
- 2 cloves garlic, minced, *optional*

1. Add all ingredients to slow cooker in the order they are listed.

2. Cover and cook on Low for 7 hours, or until meat and vegetables are tender, but not overcooked or dry.

Swiss Steak with Carrots and Tomatoes

Becky Harder, Monument, CO

Makes 6 servings

Prep. Time: 25 minutes · *Cooking Time: 5–7 hours* · *Ideal slow-cooker size: 4- or 5-qt.*

- 2-lb. lean beef round steak, cut 1-inch thick
- ¼ cup flour
- 1 tsp. kosher salt
- 1 stalk celery, chopped
- 2 carrots, pared and chopped
- ¼ cup chopped onions
- ½ tsp. Worcestershire sauce
- 2 cups whole tomatoes
- ½–1 cup tomato juice
- ½ cup freshly shredded provolone or mozzarella cheese, *optional*

1. Cut steak into six serving pieces. Dredge in flour mixed with salt. Place in slow cooker.
2. Add chopped vegetables and Worcestershire sauce.
3. Pour tomatoes and juice over meat and vegetables.
4. Cover. Cook on Low 5–7 hours.
5. Just before serving, sprinkle with grated cheese, if desired.

Serving suggestion:

This would be great served with Green Beans with Bacon on page 187.

Philly Cheese Steaks

Michele Ruvola, Vestal, NY

Makes 6 servings

Prep. Time: 15 minutes · *Cooking Time: 11 minutes*

4 cloves garlic, minced
3 tsp. freshly chopped parsley
3 tsp. freshly chopped oregano
2 tsp. freshly chopped basil
1½ tsp. sugar
1 tsp. onion powder
1 tsp. salt
½ tsp freshly chopped thyme
½ tsp. black pepper
½ tsp. paprika
¼ tsp. red pepper flakes
⅛ tsp. celery seed
1 cup beef broth
2½ lb. thinly sliced steak
1 red pepper, sliced
1 green pepper, sliced
1 onion, sliced
6 slices provolone cheese
6 hoagie rolls

1. Mix the first 12 ingredients with the beef broth in the inner pot of the Instant Pot. Place the steak slices into the liquid and top with the pepper and onion slices.
2. Seal the lid, make sure vent is at sealing. Manually set the cook time for 6 minutes on high pressure.
3. When cook time is up, let the pressure release naturally for 10 minutes, then manually release the remaining pressure.
4. Scoop meat and vegetables into rolls.
5. Top with provolone cheese and put on a baking sheet.
6. Broil in oven for 5 minutes.
7. Pour remaining juice in pot into cups for dipping.

Stuffed Cabbage

Hope Comerford, Clinton Township, MI

Makes 12–15 rolls

Prep. Time: 30 minutes ✿ *Cooking Time: 20 minutes*

- 12 cups water
- 1 large head cabbage (you will use about 12–15 leaves)
- 1 lb. 95%-fat-free ground beef
- 1 medium onion, chopped
- 2 cloves garlic, chopped
- 1 tsp. chopped fresh parsley
- ¼ tsp. salt
- ½ tsp. pepper
- 1 egg, beaten
- ¾ cup brown rice, uncooked
- 1 cup water
- 1 Tbsp. vinegar
- 16 oz. homemade pasta sauce, *divided* (see page 158)
- ¼ cup freshly chopped parsley, *divided*
- ¼ cup freshly chopped basil, *divided*
- 3 tsp. freshly chopped oregano, *divided*

1. Pour the water into the inner pot and press Sauté on the Instant Pot. Bring the water to a boil.
2. Gently lower the cabbage into the water and cook for about 5 minutes, turning to be sure all the outer leaves are softened. Press Cancel.
3. Remove the cabbage and carefully drain the water. Peel off 12 to 15 leaves.
4. In a bowl, mix the beef, onion, garlic, parsley, salt, pepper, egg, and brown rice with a wooden spoon or clean hands.
5. On a clean surface, lay out the cabbage leaves. (You may need to thin some of the thicker ribs of the cabbage leaves with a paring knife.) Evenly divide the filling among the leaves. Roll them burrito style, tucking in the ends and rolling tightly. If you need to, you can use a toothpick to hold them closed.
6. Pour the water and vinegar into the inner pot. Gently place the cabbage rolls into the pot, pouring a little sauce on top of each layer and finishing with a layer of sauce. Sprinkle with parsley, basil, and oregano.
7. Secure the lid and set the vent to sealing.
8. Set the Instant Pot to cook manually for 20 minutes on high pressure.
9. When the cook time is over, let the pressure release naturally for 20 minutes and then manually release the remaining pressure.
10. When the pin drops, remove the lid. Serve each roll hot, topped with a bit of fresh parsley, basil, and oregano.

Lasagna the Instant Pot Way

Hope Comerford, Clinton Township, MI

Makes 8 servings

Prep. Time: 15 minutes · *Cooking Time: 15 minutes*

1 Tbsp. olive oil
1 lb. lean ground beef or ground turkey
½ cup chopped onion
½ tsp. salt
⅛ tsp. pepper
2 cups water
12 lasagna noodles
8 oz. cottage cheese
1 egg
¼ cup freshly chopped parsley
¼ cup freshly chopped basil
2 tsp. freshly chopped oregano
4 cups spinach, chopped or torn
1 cup sliced mushrooms
28 oz. homemade pasta sauce (see page 158)
1 cup freshly shredded mozzarella cheese

1. Set the Instant Pot to the Sauté function and heat the olive oil. Brown the beef and onion with the salt and pepper. This will take about 5 minutes. Because you're using extra-lean ground beef, there should not be much grease, but if so, you'll need to drain it before continuing. Remove half of the ground beef and set aside. Press Cancel.

2. Pour in the water.

3. Break 4 noodles in half and arrange them on top of the beef and water.

4. Mix together the cottage cheese, egg, parsley, basil, and oregano until the mixture is smooth. Smooth half of this mixture over the lasagna noodles.

5. Layer half of the spinach and half of the mushrooms on top.

6. Break 4 more noodles in half and lay them on top of what you just did. Spread out the remaining cottage cheese mixture and layer remaining ground beef on top.

7. Layer on the remaining spinach and mushrooms, then pour half of the pasta sauce over the top.

8. Finish with breaking the remaining 4 noodles in half and laying them on top of the previous layer. Spread the remaining pasta sauce on top.

9. Secure the lid and set the vent to sealing. Manually set the cook time for 7 minutes on high pressure.

10. When the cook time is over, let the pressure release naturally for 10 minutes, then manually release the remaining pressure.

11. When the pin drops, remove the lid and sprinkle the mozzarella cheese on top. Re-cover for 5 minutes.

12. When the 5 minutes is up, remove the lid. You can let this sit for a while to thicken up on Keep Warm.

Beef and Zucchini Casserole

Judi Manos, West Islip, NY

Makes 6 servings

Prep. Time: 12 minutes & Cooking Time: 22 minutes

2 tsp. canola oil

½ cup finely chopped onion

3 cloves garlic, minced

1 lb. lean ground beef

1 lb. (3 small) zucchini, cut into ¼-inch-thick slices

¼ lb. fresh mushrooms, sliced

2 cups diced tomatoes

1½ tsp. freshly chopped oregano

1 cup brown rice

2 cups water

¼ cup freshly grated Parmesan cheese

1. Set the Instant Pot to Sauté and heat the oil in the inner pot.
2. Sauté the onion and garlic for about 3 minutes, then add the ground beef and sauté for about 8 more minutes, or until the beef is no longer pink.
3. Press Cancel. Add the remaining ingredients, except for the grated Parmesan cheese, into the inner pot in the order shown.
4. Secure the lid and set the vent to sealing.
5. Manually set the cook time for 22 minutes on high pressure.
6. When the cooking time is over, let the pressure release naturally.
7. When the pin drops, remove the lid and stir in the Parmesan cheese. Serve and enjoy!

Stuffed Bell Peppers

Mary Puterbaugh, Elwood, IN

Makes 8 servings

Prep. Time: 20 minutes ⁂ *Cooking Time: 5–11 hours* ⁂ *Ideal slow-cooker size: 6- to 7-qt.*

2 lb. ground beef, lightly browned
1 large onion, chopped
1 cup cooked rice
2 eggs, beaten
½ cup milk
½ cup ketchup
Dash hot pepper sauce
2 tsp. salt
½ tsp. pepper
8 large bell peppers, capped and seeded

1. Combine all ingredients except peppers. Gently pack mixture into peppers. Arrange the packed peppers into the greased crock.

2. Cover. Cook on Low 9–11 hours, or on High 5–6 hours.

Bacon, Spinach, and Parmesan Stuffed Meatloaf

Hope Comerford, Clinton Township, MI

Makes 4–6 servings

Prep. Time: 25 minutes · *Cooking Time: 6–7 hours* · *Ideal slow-cooker size: 4-qt.*

2 lb. lean ground beef
¾ cup cooked quinoa
¼ cup fresh minced onion
3 cloves garlic, minced
1½ tsp. onion powder
¼ cup freshly chopped parsley
¼ cup freshly chopped basil
2 tsp. freshly chopped oregano
1 egg
6 slices bacon
2 cups fresh spinach leaves
1 cup freshly shredded Parmesan cheese

1. In a bowl, mix the ground beef, quinoa, minced onion, garlic, onion powder, parsley, basil, oregano, and egg. Form into a loaf.

2. Place a piece of wax paper on your counter about 2 ft. long. Place the loaf on the wax paper and form it into a ¼-½–inch-thick rectangle.

3. Leaving about an inch on all sides, layer on the bacon, spinach leaves, and Parmesan cheese.

4. To roll up: Gently pull up on end of the wax paper so that one of the short ends starts to lift. Keep pulling it so that it starts to fold in, pressing it along the way and helping to form it into a roll. When the loaf is all rolled, seal up the ends the best you can.

5. Spray crock with nonstick spray, then place the stuffed loaf inside.

6. Cover and cook on Low for 6–7 hours.

7. Let it cool slightly before slicing.

Serving suggestions:

This would be great served alongside Bacon Ranch Red Potatoes on page 177 and Brussels Sprouts with Maple Glaze on page 180.

Meatless

Mushroom Risotto

Hope Comerford, Clinton Township, MI

Makes 4 servings

Prep. Time: 7 minutes *Cooking Time: 6 minutes*

1 Tbsp. extra-virgin olive oil
½ cup finely chopped onion
2 cloves garlic, minced
½ cup chopped baby bella mushrooms
½ cup chopped shiitake mushrooms
¼ tsp. salt
⅛ tsp. pepper
1 cup uncooked arborio rice
2 cups vegetable stock
½ cup fresh peas
¼ cup freshly grated Parmesan cheese
1 Tbsp. butter, *optional*

1. Set the Instant Pot to the Sauté function and heat the oil in the inner pot.
2. Sauté the onion and garlic for 3 minutes. Add the mushrooms, salt, and pepper, and continue sautéing for an additional 3 to 4 minutes.
3. Press Cancel. Stir in the rice and vegetable stock. Secure the lid and set the vent to sealing.
4. Manually set the cook time for 6 minutes on high pressure.
5. When the cooking time is over, manually release the pressure.
6. When the pin drops, remove the lid and stir in the peas, grated Parmesan, and butter. Let the peas heat through for about 2 minutes, then serve.

Quinoa with Spinach

Karen Ceneviva, New Haven, CT

Makes 4 servings

Prep. Time: 2 minutes ❧ *Cooking Time: 1 minute*

1½ cups raw quinoa
2¼ cups water
3 Tbsp. freshly squeezed lemon juice
2 Tbsp. extra-virgin olive oil
¼ tsp. sea salt
Pepper to taste, *optional*
2 cups fresh spinach leaves, well washed, dried, and chopped
3 large green onions, thinly sliced
3 Tbsp. fresh chopped dill

1. Rinse and drain the quinoa.
2. Pour the quinoa and water into the inner pot of the Instant Pot. Secure the lid and set the vent to sealing.
3. Manually set the time for 1 minute on high pressure.
4. When the cooking time is over, let the pressure release naturally.
5. When the pin drops, remove the lid. Stir in the lemon juice, olive oil, sea salt, and pepper (if using).
6. Stir in the spinach, green onions, and dill.
7. Serve warm, or at room temperature.

Vegetables and Red Quinoa Casserole

Gladys Voth, Hesston, KS

Makes 6–8 servings

Prep. Time: 20 minutes · *Cooking Time: 1½–4 hours* · *Ideal slow-cooker size: 4-qt.*

- 4 cups peeled and cubed butternut squash (¾-inch in size)
- 2 cups peeled and cubed beets (¾-inch in size)
- 2 cups sliced celery (½-inch thick), about 2 stalks
- 6 cloves garlic
- 1½ cups vegetable broth
- 1 cup uncooked red quinoa, rinsed and drained
- ½ cup freshly chopped basil
- Mixed berry yogurt, for topping
- ½ cup cashews, for topping

1. Grease interior of crock.
2. Place butternut squash, beets, and celery in crock.
3. Coarsely chop garlic cloves. Place in crock.
4. Pour vegetable broth over ingredients in slow cooker. Stir.
5. Cover. Cook on High 1½–2 hours, or on Low 3–4 hours.
6. About 30 minutes before end of cooking time, stir in quinoa. Cover and cook on High 20–30 minutes.
7. When cook time is up, uncover and stir in the basil.
8. Serve hot or at room temperature and top each serving with the yogurt and a sprinkling of cashews.

Batilgian

Donna Treloar, Muncie, IN

Makes 4–6 servings

Prep. Time: 15–20 minutes · *Cooking Time: 3 hours* · *Ideal slow-cooker size: 5- or 6-qt.*

- 1 large Spanish onion, diced
- 5 Tbsp. olive oil, *divided*
- 4 celery ribs, cut in 1-inch pieces
- 2 cups fresh green beans, trimmed, cut in 2-inch pieces
- 3 bay leaves
- 3 cloves garlic, pressed
- 2 Tbsp. finely chopped fresh basil
- 1 large eggplant, cubed
- Salt and pepper to taste
- 28-oz. can chopped tomatoes
- 2 Tbsp. fresh lemon juice
- 2 Tbsp. capers, *optional*

1. In a large skillet, sauté onion in 3 Tbsp. olive oil.
2. Add celery. Cover and cook 5 minutes.
3. Add green beans, bay leaves, garlic, basil, and eggplant. Cover and cook 7 minutes.
4. Transfer mixture to slow cooker.
5. Sprinkle with salt and pepper. Drizzle remaining 2 Tbsp. oil over the contents of the crock.
6. Top with tomatoes.
7. Cover and cook on Low 3 hours, stirring gently once or twice.
8. Remove bay leaves. Add lemon juice and capers if you wish, just before serving.

Serving suggestion:
Serve alongside your favorite crusty bread.

Summer Squash Pie

Natalia Showalter, Mount Solon, VA

Makes 4 main-dish servings

Prep. Time: 20 minutes ❧ *Cooking Time: 25 minutes* ❧ *Standing Time: 10 minutes*

- 3 cups shredded summer squash
- 2 Tbsp. olive oil
- ½ cup chopped onion
- ½ cup shredded carrot
- 3 cloves garlic, minced
- 2 egg whites
- ½ cup sour cream
- ¾ cup freshly shredded mozzarella cheese
- 2 Tbsp. fresh minced parsley
- ¾ tsp. freshly chopped oregano
- ¼ tsp. pepper
- ½ cup cracker crumbs
- 1½ cups water

1. Place the shredded squash into a clean cloth kitchen towel. Fold the towel over the squash and twist or press the towel to remove moisture.
2. Set the Instant Pot to Sauté and heat the oil in the inner pot.
3. Sauté the squash, onion, carrot, and garlic in the heated olive oil for about 8 minutes. Hit Cancel.
4. In a bowl, mix the egg whites, sour cream, cheese, parsley, oregano, and pepper. Stir in the sautéed vegetables.
5. Pour into 7-inch round pan or baking dish.
6. Garnish the top with cracker crumbs.
7. Wipe out the inner pot with a paper towel.
8. Pour the water into the inner pot. Place the trivet on top.
9. Place the filled round pan/baking dish on top of the trivet.
10. Secure the lid and set the vent to sealing.
11. Manually set the cook time to 25 minutes.
12. When the cooking time is over, manually release the pressure.
13. When the pin drops, remove the lid. Carefully remove the trivet and pan/dish with oven mitts. Allow to stand 10 minutes before cutting.

Pasta Primavera

Hope Comerford, Clinton Township, MI

Makes 6 servings

Prep. Time: 10 minutes ❧ *Cooking Time: 5 minutes (may vary due to pasta chosen)*

- 2 cups chopped broccolini tops
- ½ lb. baby bella mushrooms, sliced
- 2 small zucchini, sliced into ¼-inch-thick rounds
- 1 cup sliced cherry tomatoes
- 3 cloves garlic, sliced
- ½ tsp. salt
- ⅛ tsp. pepper
- 2 Tbsp. olive oil, *divided*
- 8 oz. pasta of your choice
- 4 cups vegetable stock
- ¼ cup freshly grated Parmesan cheese
- 2 Tbsp. chopped fresh basil

1. In a large bowl, toss the broccolini, mushrooms, zucchini, cherry tomatoes, garlic, salt, and pepper with 1 Tbsp. olive oil.
2. Set the Instant Pot to Sauté and heat the additional Tbsp. of olive oil.
3. Pour the vegetables into the inner pot. Stir regularly for about 7 minutes, or until the vegetables are tender. Put them back in the large bowl you had them in and cover to keep them warm.
4. Press Cancel on the Instant Pot. Pour the pasta and vegetable stock into the inner pot and secure the lid. Set the vent to sealing.
5. Manually set the cook time for 5 minutes on high pressure, or half of whatever time the package instructions say to cook your pasta of choice.
6. When the cooking time is over, manually release the pressure.
7. When the pin drops, remove the lid. Use a ladle to remove 1 cup of the cooking liquid. Pour this into the bowl with vegetables.
8. Wearing oven mitts, carefully remove the inner pot and drain the pasta into a colander.
9. Pour the drained pasta into the large bowl with the reserved cooking liquid and vegetables. Add the Parmesan cheese and fresh basil. Toss and enjoy!

Fresh Veggie Lasagna

Deanne Gingrich, Lancaster, PA

Makes 4–6 servings

Prep. Time: 30 minutes ⁂ *Cooking Time: 4 hours* ⁂ *Ideal slow-cooker size: 4- or 5-qt.*

1½ cups freshly shredded mozzarella cheese
½ cup ricotta cheese
⅓ cup freshly grated Parmesan cheese
1 egg, lightly beaten
3 tsp. freshly chopped oregano
1 clove garlic, minced
3 cups fresh pasta sauce, *divided* (see page 158)
1 medium zucchini, diced, *divided*
4 uncooked lasagna noodles
4 cups fresh baby spinach, *divided*
1 cup fresh mushrooms, sliced, *divided*

1. Grease interior of slow-cooker crock.
2. In a bowl, mix the mozzarella, ricotta, and Parmesan cheese, egg, oregano, and garlic. Set aside.
3. Spread ½ cup pasta sauce in crock.
4. Sprinkle with half the zucchini.
5. Spoon ⅓ of cheese mixture over zucchini.
6. Break 2 noodles into large pieces to cover cheese layer.
7. Spread ½ cup pasta sauce over noodles.
8. Top with half the spinach and then half the mushrooms.
9. Repeat layers, ending with cheese mixture, and then sauce. Press layers down firmly.
10. Cover and cook on Low for 4 hours, or until vegetables are as tender as you like them and noodles are fully cooked.
11. Let stand 15 minutes so lasagna can firm up before serving.

Cherry Tomato Pasta Sauce

Beverly Hummel, Fleetwood, PA

Makes 8–10 servings

Prep. Time: 20 minutes · *Cooking Time: 4–5 hours* · *Ideal slow-cooker size: 6-qt.*

4 qt. cherry tomatoes
1 onion, chopped
2 cloves garlic, minced
3 tsp. sugar
3 tsp. freshly chopped rosemary
1½ Tbsp. freshly chopped thyme
3 tsp. freshly chopped oregano
3 tsp. freshly chopped basil
1 tsp. salt
½ tsp. coarsely ground black pepper

1. Grease interior of slow-cooker crock.
2. Stem tomatoes and cut them in half. Place in slow cooker.
3. Add chopped onion and garlic to cooker.
4. Stir in sugar, herbs, and seasonings, mixing well.
5. Cover. Cook on Low 4–5 hours, or until the veggies are as tender as you like them.
6. For a thicker sauce, uncover the cooker for the last 30–60 minutes of cooking time.

Serving suggestion:

Serve over fresh pasta or use in any recipe which requires pasta sauce.

Seafood

Twisted Shrimp Scampi à la Mamma Ree

Maria Shevlin, Sicklerville, NJ

Makes 4–6 servings
Prep. Time: 30 minutes *Cooking Time: 20 minutes*

2 Tbsp. butter
1 Tbsp. olive oil
3 Tbsp. finely chopped garlic
1 cup vegetable broth
¼ cup white wine, or broth
¼ cup freshly chopped parsley
¼ cup freshly chopped basil
2 tsp. freshly chopped oregano
1 tsp. garlic powder
½ tsp. black pepper
Pinch to 1 tsp. red pepper flakes, *optional* (you may use much less if you prefer as well)
1 medium onion, cut into thin strips
2 red bell peppers, cut into thin strips
1–1½ lb. large shrimp
Cornstarch for dredging

1. Set the Instant Pot to the Sauté function and let it get hot. Add the butter, oil, and chopped garlic to the bottom of the inner pot and sauté for approximately 1 minute, or until butter melts.
2. Add the broth, wine, and all seasonings.
3. Once brought to a nice simmer, add the onion and bell pepper strips.
4. Simmer, approximately 10 minutes.
5. Meanwhile peel and devein the shrimp and ever so lightly, dredge the shrimp in cornstarch. Shake to remove excess.
6. Add the shrimp directly to the simmering Instant Pot, and push gently into the liquid and veggies.
7. Cook for 3–4 minutes.
8. Stir and simmer for another 3–5 minutes.

Serving suggestion:

Serve over rice, spaghetti, or fettuccine-style pasta.

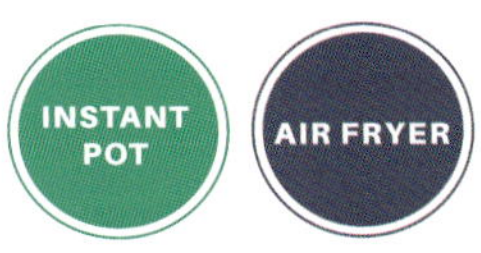

Honey Lemon Garlic Salmon

Judy Gascho, Woodburn, OR

Makes 4 servings
Prep. Time: 15 minutes *Cooking Time: 8 minutes*

5 Tbsp. olive oil
3 Tbsp. honey
2–3 Tbsp. fresh lemon juice
3 cloves minced, garlic
4 (3–4-oz.) fresh salmon fillets
Salt and pepper to taste
4 Tbsp. fresh minced parsley
Lemon slices, *optional*

1. Mix olive oil, honey, lemon juice, and minced garlic in a bowl.
2. Place each salmon fillet on a piece of foil big enough to wrap up the piece of fish.
3. Brush each fillet generously with the olive oil mixture.
4. Sprinkle with salt, pepper, and parsley flakes.
5. Top each with a thin slice of lemon if desired.
6. Wrap each fillet and seal well at top.
7. Place 1 ½ cups of water in the inner pot of your Instant Pot and place the trivet in the pot.
8. Place wrapped fillets on the trivet.
9. Close the lid and turn valve to sealing.
10. Cook on manual at high pressure for 5 to 8 minutes for smaller pieces, or for 10 to 12 minutes if they are large.
11. Carefully release pressure at the end of the cooking time manually.
12. Unwrap and enjoy.

Air Fryer Adaptation:

1. Preheat the air fryer to 400°F.
2. Mix olive oil, honey, lemon juice, and minced garlic in a bowl.
3. Brush each fillet generously with the olive oil mixture.
4. Sprinkle with salt and pepper.
5. Top each with a thin slice of lemon if desired.
6. Arrange the salmon fillets in the air fryer basket.
7. Air fry for 7–9 minutes at 400°F, then check for doneness.
8. Serve each fillet with a sprinkling of minced parsley.

Serving suggestion:

This would be great served with Lemony Garlic Asparagus on page 195.

Salmon with Chives

Gloria Julien, Gladstone, MI

Makes 2 servings

Prep. Time: 5 minutes · *Cooking Time: 3–5 minutes*

1 cup water
2 (5-oz.) pieces salmon with skin
2 tsp. extra-virgin olive oil
1 Tbsp. chopped chives
1 Tbsp. fresh tarragon leaves, *optional*

Serving suggestions:
This would be great served with Steamed Veggie Medley on page 193 and Spicy Roasted Butternut Squash on page 179.

1. Pour the water into the inner pot of the Instant Pot and place the trivet on top.
2. Line a 7-inch round baking pan with foil.
3. Rub the salmon all over with the oil.
4. Place the salmon skin-side down on the foil. Place the baking pan on top of the trivet in the inner pot.
5. Secure the lid and set the vent to sealing.
6. Manually set the cook time on high pressure for 3 minutes if fresh or 5 minutes if frozen.
7. When the cooking time is over, manually release the pressure.
8. When the pin drops, remove the lid and carefully remove the trivet from the inner pot with oven mitts. Check to make sure the fillet is at 145°F.
9. Using a metal spatula, lift salmon off skin and place salmon on serving plate. Discard skin.
10. Sprinkle salmon with herbs and serve.

Air Fryer Adaptation:

1. Preheat the air fryer to 400°F.
2. Rub the salmon all over with the oil.
3. Place the salmon skin-side down in the air fryer basket.
4. Air fry for 7–9 minutes at 400°F, then check for doneness. Cook for an additional 1–2 minutes if needed.
5. Serve each fillet with the fresh herbs sprinkled over the top.

Greek-Style Halibut Steaks

Kristi See, Weskan, KS

Makes 4 servings

Prep. Time: 10 minutes · *Cooking Time: 3 minutes*

- 1 tsp. olive oil
- 1 cup unpeeled diced zucchini
- ½ cup minced onion
- 1 clove garlic, peeled and minced
- 2 cups diced fresh tomatoes
- 2 Tbsp. chopped fresh basil
- ¼ tsp. salt
- ¼ tsp. pepper
- 4 (6-oz.) halibut steaks or other white flaky fish
- ⅓ cup crumbled feta cheese
- 1 cup water

1. Set the Instant Pot to the Sauté function and heat the olive oil in the inner pot.
2. Sauté the zucchini, onion, and garlic for 5 minutes.
3. Mix in the tomatoes, basil, salt, and pepper. Press Cancel.
4. In a 7-inch round baking pan, arrange the halibut steaks. Using oven mitts, carefully pour the zucchini mixture from the inner pot over the halibut. Top with the feta cheese.
5. Quickly wipe out the inner pot. Pour in the water and place the trivet on top.
6. Place the baking pan on top of the trivet in the inner pot. Secure the lid and set the vent to sealing.
7. Manually set the cook time for 3 minutes on high pressure.
8. When the cooking time is over, manually release the pressure.
9. When the pin drops, remove the lid and carefully take the trivet out with oven mitts. Make sure the fish has reached 145°F. Serve halibut and enjoy!

Serving suggestion:

These would be great served alongside Garden Chips on page 190.

Herbed Fish Fillets

Patricia Howard, Green Valley, AZ

Makes 4 servings

Prep. Time: 5 minutes ⁂ *Cooking Time: 5–9 minutes*

- 1 cup water
- 4 fish fillets (hake, cod, or mahi-mahi), fresh or frozen
- Juice of ½ lemon
- 1 tsp. no-salt seasoning
- 3 tsp. freshly chopped dill weed
- 3 tsp. freshly chopped basil
- 3 tsp. freshly chopped parsley
- 4 thin slices lemon

Serving suggestions:

These would be great served with Steamed Veggie Medley on page 193 and Rosemary Carrots on page 185.

1. Pour the water into the inner pot of the Instant Pot and place the trivet on top.

2. Arrange the fillets in a 7-inch round baking pan. It's all right if they overlap a bit.

3. In a small bowl, mix the lemon juice, no-salt seasoning, dill, basil, and parsley. Pour this over the fillets and place a slice of lemon on top of each fillet.

4. Secure the lid and set the vent to sealing.

5. Manually set the cook time for 5 minutes on high pressure for fresh fish, or 9 minutes for frozen fish.

6. When the cooking time is over, manually release the pressure.

7. When the pin drops, remove the lid. Make sure the fish is at 145°F.

Side Dishes

Quinoa with Vegetables

Hope Comerford, Clinton Township, MI

Makes 4–6 servings

Prep. Time: 10 minutes ❧ *Cooking Time: 4–6 hours* ❧ *Ideal slow-cooker size: 3-qt.*

- 2 cups quinoa
- 4 cups vegetable stock
- ½ cup chopped onion
- 1 Tbsp. olive oil
- 1 medium red pepper, chopped
- 1 medium yellow pepper, chopped
- 1 medium carrot, chopped
- 3 cloves garlic, minced
- ½ tsp. sea salt
- ¼ tsp. pepper
- 1 Tbsp. fresh cilantro, chopped

1. Place quinoa, vegetable stock, onion, olive oil, red pepper, yellow pepper, carrot, garlic, salt, and pepper into crock and stir.

2. Cook on Low for 4–6 hours or until liquid is absorbed and quinoa is tender.

3. Top with fresh cilantro to serve.

Veggie Loaded Rice

Maria Shevlin, Sicklerville, NJ

Makes 4–6 servings

Prep. Time: 10 minutes ⁂ *Cooking Time: 11–13 minutes*

- 1 Tbsp. olive oil
- 2–3 cloves garlic, minced
- ½ medium onion, chopped fine
- ½ cup carrot, shredded
- ¼ cup red bell pepper, chopped fine
- ½ cup mushrooms, chopped fine
- ½ cup zucchini, shredded
- 2 cups cooked rice, warmed
- ½ cup vegetable stock
- 1 tsp. salt
- ¼ tsp. onion powder
- ½ tsp. black pepper
- 1–2 pinches red pepper flakes
- 1 Tbsp. fresh parsley, chopped fine
- 2 tsp. fresh basil, chiffonade

1. Set the Instant Pot to Sauté and add the oil to heat.
2. Sauté the garlic, onion, carrot, and bell pepper for 3–5 minutes, stirring frequently.
3. Add the mushrooms and zucchini and stir until mixed.
4. Press Cancel. Add the rice, stock, and seasonings. Mix well, taste, and adjust salt and pepper if needed.
5. Stir in the fresh herbs.

Serving suggestions:

- Serve as a main course or side dish to chicken, pork, or beef. You can even add in cooked shrimp and a couple of scrambled eggs for a shrimp & veggie fried rice–style meal.
- This would also be great served alongside Four-Pepper Steak on page 134.

Cilantro Lime Rice

Cindy Herren, West Des Moines, IA

Makes 6–8 servings
Prep. Time: 5 minutes · *Cooking Time: 3 minutes*

2 cups extra-long grain rice or jasmine rice
4 cups water
2 Tbsp. olive oil or butter, *divided*
2 tsp. salt
¼ cup fresh chopped cilantro
1 lime, juiced

1. Add the rice, the water, 1 Tbsp. of the oil, and the salt to the inner pot of the Instant Pot and stir.
2. Secure the lid and set the vent to sealing.
3. Manually set the cook time to 3 minutes on high pressure.
4. When the cooking time is over, let the pressure release naturally for 10 minutes, then manually release the remaining pressure.
5. When the pin drops, remove the lid. Fluff the rice with a fork. Add the chopped cilantro, lime juice, and remaining oil and mix well.

Serving suggestion:
This would be great served alongside Carnitas on page 113.

Thyme Roasted Sweet Potatoes

Hope Comerford, Clinton Township, MI

Makes 6 servings

Prep. Time: 20 minutes ❧ *Cooking Time: 7 hours* ❧ *Ideal slow-cooker size: 4-qt.*

4 medium sweet potatoes, peeled, cubed

3 Tbsp. olive oil

5–6 large cloves garlic, minced

⅓ cup fresh thyme leaves

½ tsp. kosher salt

¼ tsp. red pepper flakes

Serving suggestion:

These would go well served with Garlic Mushroom Thighs on page 88 and Thyme and Garlic Turkey Breast on page 90.

1. Place all ingredients into the crock and stir.
2. Cover and cook on low for 7 hours, or until potatoes are tender.

Air Fryer Adaptation:

1. Preheat to 400°F for 5 minutes.
2. Coat the sweet potato cubes with the olive oil, garlic, thyme, salt, and red pepper flakes.
3. Place enough of the sweet potatoes into the basket to create a single layer. You do not want to overcrowd the basket, so cook in 2–3 batches.
4. Cook on 400°F for 15 minutes, shaking the basket every 5 minutes.
5. If the potatoes are still not tender when you poke them with a fork, cook for an additional 2–3 minutes, or until they are soft inside.

Aunt Twila's Beans

Mary Louise Martin, Boyd, WI

Makes 10–12 servings

Prep. Time: 15 minutes ⁂ *Cooking Time: 10 hours* ⁂ *Ideal slow-cooker size: 5-qt.*

5 cups dry pinto beans
2 tsp. ground cumin
1 medium yellow onion, minced
4 cloves garlic, minced
9 cups water
3 tsp. salt
3 Tbsp. fresh lemon juice

1. Combine beans, cumin, onion, garlic, and water in slow cooker.
2. Cook on Low for 8 hours.
3. Add salt and lemon juice. Stir. Cook on Low for another 2 hours.

Serving suggestions:

This would be great served with Jazzed-Up Barbecue Pulled Chicken on page 106 and Tender and Tangy Ribs on page 116.

Potatoes with Parsley

Colleen Heatwole, Burton, MI

Makes 4 servings

Prep. Time: 10 minutes · *Cooking Time: 5 minutes*

3 Tbsp. olive oil, *divided*

2 lb. medium red potatoes, (about 2 oz. each) halved lengthwise

1 clove garlic, minced

½ tsp. salt

½ cup vegetable broth

2 Tbsp. chopped fresh parsley

1. Place 1 Tbsp. olive in the inner pot of the Instant Pot and select sauté.
2. When olive oil is hot, add potatoes, garlic, and salt, stirring well.
3. Sauté for 4 minutes, stirring frequently.
4. Add vegetable broth and stir well.
5. Seal lid, make sure vent is on sealing, then select manual for 5 minutes on High.
6. When cooking time is up, manually release the pressure.
7. Strain potatoes toss with remaining 2 Tbsp. olive oil and chopped parsley. Serve immediately.

Air Fryer Adaptation:

1. Place the potato pieces into a bowl of warm water for 15 minutes. After the 15 minutes, drain the water and pat the pieces completely dry.
2. Preheat the air fryer to 400°F.
3. Coat the potato pieces with the all of the olive oil, garlic, and salt. (Omit the vegetable broth.)
4. Place the potato pieces into the basket and cook on 400°F for 20 minutes, shaking the basket every 5 minutes.
5. If the potatoes are not crispy enough for you, place them back in to cook an additional 5–10 minutes.
6. Sprinkle with the parsley before serving.

Bacon Ranch Red Potatoes

Hope Comerford, Clinton Township, MI

Makes 6 servings

Prep. Time: 15 minutes · *Cooking Time: 7 minutes*

- 4 strips bacon, chopped into small pieces
- 2 lb. red potatoes, diced
- 1 Tbsp. fresh chopped parsley
- 1 tsp. sea salt
- 4 cloves garlic, chopped
- 1-oz. packet ranch dressing/seasoning mix
- ⅓ cup water
- ½ cup freshly shredded sharp white cheddar
- 2 Tbsp. chopped green onions, for garnish

1. Set the Instant Pot to Sauté, add the bacon to the inner pot, and cook until crisp.
2. Stir in the potatoes, parsley, sea salt, garlic, ranch dressing seasoning, and water.
3. Secure the lid, make sure vent is at sealing, then set the Instant Pot to Manual for 7 minutes at high pressure.
4. When cooking time is up, do a quick release and carefully open the lid.
5. Stir in the cheese. Garnish with the green onions.

Serving suggestion:

These would be great served alongside Bacon, Spinach, and Parmesan Stuffed Meatloaf on page 145.

Best Smashed Potatoes

Colleen Heatwole, Burton, MI

Makes 12 servings

Prep. Time: 30 minutes ❧ *Cooking Time: 5–6 hours* ❧ *Ideal slow-cooker size: 5½-qt.*

- 5 lb. potatoes, cooked, peeled, mashed, or riced
- 8 oz. cream cheese, at room temperature
- 1½ cups nonfat plain Greek yogurt, at room temperature
- 3 cloves garlic, minced
- 2½ tsp. salt
- ¼ tsp. pepper
- 2 Tbsp. butter

1. Combine all ingredients in slow cooker.
2. Cover. Cook on Low 5–6 hours.

Serving suggestion:

These would go well with Garlic and Lemon Chicken on page 87.

Spicy Roasted Butternut Squash

Marilyn Mowry, Irving, TX

Makes 15–20 servings

Prep. Time: 1 hour ⁂ *Cooking Time: 4–6 hours* ⁂ *Ideal slow-cooker size: 6-qt.*

¼ cup olive oil
2 tsp. ground cinnamon, *divided*
½ tsp. ground cumin
1¾ tsp. salt, *divided*
5 lb. butternut squash, split in quarters and seeds removed
2 carrots, diced
1 large white onion, diced
2 Granny Smith apples, peeled, cored, and quartered
4 chipotles in adobo sauce, seeds scraped out, chopped
Roughly 10 cups chicken stock

Serving suggestion:
This would be great served alongside Salmon with Chives on page 163.

1. Mix olive oil, 1 tsp. cinnamon, ground cumin, and ¾ tsp. salt in mixing bowl. Brush over the flesh of the quartered squash.

2. Place squash cut side down on a rimmed baking sheet lined with foil.

3. Add carrots, onion, and apples to bowl with oil and toss. Spread on another foil-lined sheet.

4. Roast both trays 40–50 minutes at 425°F until squash is soft and onion mix is golden brown. Scoop out the squash.

5. Put squash, veggie mix, chipotles, 1 tsp. salt, and 1 tsp. cinnamon in slow cooker. Add chicken broth.

6. Cover and cook on High 4 hours or Low for 6 hours. Mash with a potato masher or puree with immersion blender.

Brussels Sprouts with Maple Glaze

Hope Comerford, Clinton Township, MI

Makes 6 servings
Prep. Time: 5–6 minutes · *Cook Time: 3 minutes*

- 4 slices thick-cut bacon, chopped into ½-inch pieces
- 1 shallot, chopped
- ½ cup chicken broth
- 1 lb. brussels sprouts, halved (quartered if large)
- ⅓ cup light brown sugar
- 1½ Tbsp. Dijon mustard
- 2 Tbsp. maple syrup

1. Set the Instant Pot to the Sauté function and let it get nice and hot. Spray the inner pot with nonstick cooking spray and then add the bacon. Sauté until crispy.
2. Add the shallot and sauté for 1 more minute.
3. Pour in the chicken broth and scrape the bottom of the pot with a wooden spoon or spatula. Press Cancel.
4. Pour in the brussels sprouts and secure the lid. Set the vent to sealing.
5. Manually set the cook time for 3 minutes. When the cook time is over, manually release the pressure.
6. When the pin drops, remove the lid.
7. In a medium bowl, mix the brown sugar, Dijon mustard, and maple syrup.
8. Remove the contents of the inner pot with a slotted spoon into the bowl with the maple glaze. Toss and serve.

Air Fryer Adaptation:

1. Preheat the air fryer to 400°F for 3–5 minutes.
2. Toss the brussels sprouts, bacon, and shallot with 2 tsp. olive oil, and salt and pepper to taste.
3. Place them in the air fryer basket.
4. Air fry at 400°F for 10–15 minutes.
5. Meanwhile, mix the brown sugar, Dijon mustard, and maple syrup in a medium bowl.
6. When the brussels sprouts are done, pour the brussels sprouts into the bowl with the maple sauce and coat everything evenly. Serve.

Serving suggestion:
These would be great served alongside Bacon, Spinach, and Parmesan Stuffed Meatloaf on page 145.

Slow-Cooker Beets

Hope Comerford, Clinton Township, MI

Makes 4–6 servings

Prep. Time: 10 minutes ❧ *Cooking Time: 3–4 hours* ❧ *Ideal slow-cooker size: 3-qt.*

4–6 large beets, scrubbed well and tops removed
3 Tbsp. olive oil
1 tsp. sea salt
¼ tsp. pepper
3 Tbsp. balsamic vinegar
1 Tbsp. lemon juice

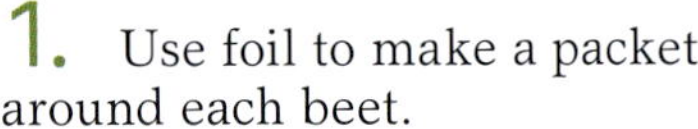

1. Use foil to make a packet around each beet.
2. Divide the olive oil, salt, pepper, balsamic vinegar, and lemon juice evenly between each packet.
3. Place each beet packet into the slow cooker.
4. Cover and cook on Low for 3–4 hours, or until the beets are tender when poked with a knife.
5. Remove each beet packet from the crock and allow to cool and let the steam escape. Once cool enough to handle, use a paring knife to gently peel the skin off each beet. Cut into bite-sized pieces and serve with juice from the packet over the top.

Instant Pot Adaptation:

1. Use foil to make a packet around each beet.
2. Divide the olive oil, salt, pepper, balsamic vinegar, and lemon juice evenly between each packet.
3. Pour 1 cup water into the inner pot of the Instant Pot and place the trivet or steamer basket on top.
4. Place each beet packet onto the trivet or into the steamer basket.
5. Secure the lid and set the vent to sealing.
6. Manually set the cook time for 16 minutes on high pressure.
7. When the cooking time is over, let the pressure release naturally for 10 minutes, then manually release the remaining pressure.
8. When the pin drops, remove the lid. Transfer the beets to a plate using tongs. Allow to cool and let the steam escape.
9. Once cool enough to handle, unwrap each beet packet and use a paring knife to gently peel the skin off each beet. Cut into bite-sized pieces and serve with juice from the packet over the top.

Serving suggestion:

These would go well served with Thyme and Garlic Turkey Breast on page 90.

Chili-Lime Corn on the Cob

Hope Comerford, Clinton Township, MI

Makes 6 servings

Prep. Time: 10 minutes · *Cooking Time: 4 hours* · *Ideal slow-cooker size: 6-qt.*

6 ears corn, shucked and cleaned
3 tsp. butter, at room temperature
2 Tbsp. freshly squeezed lime juice
1 tsp. lime zest
2 tsp. chili powder
1 tsp. salt
½ tsp. pepper

1. Tear off 6 pieces of aluminum foil to fit each ear of corn. Place each ear of corn on a piece of foil.

2. Mix together butter, lime juice, lime zest, chili powder, salt, and pepper.

3. Divide butter mixture evenly among six ears of corn and spread it over ears of corn. Wrap them tightly with foil so they don't leak.

4. Place the foil-wrapped ears of corn into crock. Cover and cook on Low for 4 hours.

Serving suggestions:

This would be great served with Jazzed-Up Barbecue Pulled Chicken on page 106 and Tender and Tangy Ribs on page 116.

Rosemary Carrots

Orpha Herr, Andover, NY

Makes 6 servings
Prep. Time: 10 minutes *Cooking Time: 2 minutes*

1 cup water
1 ½ lb. carrots, sliced
1 Tbsp. olive oil
½ cup diced green bell pepper
3 tsp. freshly minced rosemary
¼ tsp. coarsely ground black pepper

Serving suggestion:
These would be great served alongside Pork and Sweet Potatoes on page 112.

1. Pour the water into the inner pot of the Instant Pot, place the sliced carrots into a steamer basket, and put the steamer basket into the inner pot.
2. Secure the lid and set the vent to sealing.
3. Manually set the cook time for 2 minutes on high pressure.
4. When the cooking time is over, manually release the pressure. Wait for the pin to drop and remove the lid. Press Cancel.
5. Carefully remove the carrots, set aside, and empty the water out of the inner pot. Wipe dry.
6. Place the inner pot back into the Instant Pot, then press Sauté and heat the oil in the inner pot.
7. Add the green bell pepper and sauté for 5 minutes, then add the carrots and stir.
8. Sprinkle the carrots and green pepper with rosemary and black pepper. Serve and enjoy!

Orange-Glazed Carrots

Cyndie Marrara, Port Matilda, PA

Makes 6 servings

Prep. Time: 5–10 minutes · *Cooking Time: 3–4 hours* · *Ideal slow-cooker size: 3½-qt.*

- 32-oz. (2 lb.) pkg. baby carrots
- ⅓ cup turbinado sugar
- 2–3 oranges, squeezed for juice to make approx. ½ cup juice
- 3 Tbsp. coconut oil, melted
- ¾ tsp. cinnamon
- ¼ tsp. nutmeg
- 2 Tbsp. cornstarch
- ¼ cup water

1. Combine all ingredients except cornstarch and water in slow cooker.

2. Cover. Cook on low 3–4 hours, until carrots are tender crisp.

3. Put carrots in serving dish and keep warm, reserving cooking juices. Put reserved juices in small saucepan. Bring to boil.

4. Mix cornstarch and water in small bowl until blended. Add to juices. Boil one minute or until thickened, stirring constantly.

5. Pour over carrots and serve.

Serving suggestion:

These would be great served alongside Carolina Pot Roast on page 124.

Green Beans with Bacon

Hope Comerford, Clinton Township, MI

Makes 6 servings

Prep. Time: 7 minutes *Cooking Time: 5 minutes*

- 5 slices thick-cut bacon, chopped
- ½ cup chopped red onion
- 4 cloves garlic, chopped
- ¾ cups chicken stock
- ½ tsp. sea salt
- ⅛ tsp. pepper
- ⅛ tsp. red pepper flakes
- 1½ lb. fresh green beans, ends snipped and cut in half

Serving suggestion:

These would be great served alongside Swiss Steak with Carrots and Tomatoes on page 137.

1. Set the Instant Pot to the Sauté function and let it get nice and hot. Spray the inner pot with nonstick cooking spray and then add the bacon. Sauté until crispy.

2. Add the onion and garlic to the inner pot and sauté for an additional 2–3 minutes.

3. Pour in the chicken stock and scrape the bottom of the inner pot with a wooden spoon or spatula, bringing up any stuck on bits. Press Cancel.

4. Pour in the remaining ingredients.

5. Secure the lid and set the vent to sealing. Manually set the cook time for 5 minutes on high pressure.

6. When the cook time is over, manually release the pressure.

Fresh Zucchini with Bacon

Pauline Morrison, St. Marys, Ontario

Makes 6–8 servings

Prep. Time: 8 minutes *Cooking Time: 2 minutes*

1 cup water

1½ lb. zucchini, peeled if you wish, and cut into ¼-inch slices

1½ Tbsp. coconut oil

1½ cloves garlic, minced

28-oz. can stewed tomatoes, broken up

½ tsp. salt

1. Pour the water into the inner pot of the Instant Pot and place the steaming basket in the inner pot. Place the zucchini slices in the basket.
2. Secure the lid and set the vent to sealing.
3. Manually set the cook time for 2 minutes on high pressure.
4. When the cooking time is over, manually release the pressure.
5. When the pin drops, remove the lid and the steaming basket. Press Cancel.
6. Drain the water carefully from the inner pot and wipe dry.
7. Press Sauté and heat the coconut oil in the inner pot. When the oil is heated, sauté the garlic for 1 minute.
8. Add the tomatoes with their juices, garlic, salt, and zucchini. Mix well and let all the ingredients heat through, about 3–5 minutes.

Serving suggestion:

This would be great served alongside Greek-Style Halibut Steaks on page 164.

Garden Chips

MarJanita Geigley, Lancaster, PA

Makes 4 servings

Prep. Time: 15 minutes · *Cooking Time: 2 hours* · *Ideal slow-cooker size: 3- or 4-qt.*

½ cup oat flour
⅛ tsp. pepper
2 Tbsp. grated Parmesan cheese
3 egg whites
3–4 medium zucchini, cut into ¼-inch slices

Serving suggestion:
These would be great served alongside Greek-Style Halibut Steaks on page 164.

1. In small bowl mix together oat flour, pepper, and Parmesan cheese.
2. Place egg whites in another dish and whisk.
3. Dip zucchini in egg whites then into oat flour mixture.
4. Place zucchini into greased slow cooker and cook on Low for 1 hour.
5. Turn chips and cook for another hour.

Air Fryer Adaptation:

1. In small bowl, mix together oat flour, pepper, and Parmesan cheese.
2. Place egg whites in another dish and whisk.
3. Dip zucchini in egg whites then into oat flour mixture.
4. Place zucchini in a single layer into the air fryer basket. (You will need to cook these in multiple batches.)
5. Cook at 400°F for 8 minutes, flipping the zucchini over halfway through the cook time.

Broccoli and Bell Peppers

Frieda Weisz, Aberdeen, SD

Makes 8 servings

Prep. Time: 20 minutes · *Cooking Time: 4–5 hours* · *Ideal slow-cooker size: 3½- or 4-qt.*

2 lb. fresh broccoli, trimmed and chopped into bite-sized pieces

1 clove garlic, minced

1 green or red bell pepper, cut into thin slices

1 onion, peeled and cut into slices

4 Tbsp. soy sauce or Bragg Liquid Aminos

½ tsp. salt

Dash black pepper

1 Tbsp. sesame seeds, *optional*, as garnish

1. Combine all ingredients except sesame seeds in slow cooker.

2. Cook on Low for 4–5 hours. Top with sesame seeds.

Serving suggestion:

This would be great served alongside Hungarian Beef with Paprika on page 129.

Steamed Veggie Medley

Maria Shevlin, Sicklerville, NJ

Makes 6 servings

Prep. Time: 5 minutes · *Cooking Time: 2 minutes*

1 cup water
3 cups fresh cauliflower florets
16-oz. bag baby carrots, cut in half
1 Tbsp. olive oil
2 Tbsp. butter
8 oz. mushrooms, diced
1 small onion, diced
2 cloves garlic, minced
Salt to taste
Pepper to taste
½ tsp. garlic powder
2 Tbsp. fresh parsley, chopped
½ tsp. fresh thyme, chopped fine
½ tsp. fresh sage, chopped fine

1. Pour 1 cup water into the bottom of the inner pot. Place the steamer basket inside.
2. Add in the cauliflower and carrots.
3. Secure the lid and set the vent to sealing. Press Steam and set the timer to 2 minutes.
4. When cook time is up, let the pressure release naturally for 3–4 minutes, then manually release any remaining pressure.
5. When the pin drops, remove the lid, and carefully lift the steamer basket out. Drain the water from the pot and cover the veggies to keep them warm.
6. Press Sauté, then add the olive oil, butter, mushrooms, onions, and garlic to the inner pot.
7. Sauté until the veggies are cooked, then press Cancel. Add the steamed cauliflower and carrots in and toss together.
8. Season with salt, pepper, and garlic powder.
9. Top with the fresh herbs and toss gently.

Serving suggestions:

This would go well served with Herbed Chicken on page 42, Salmon with Chives on page 163, and Herbed Fish Fillets on page 166.

Garlic Butter Cauliflower

Hope Comerford, Clinton Township, MI

Makes 6–8 servings

Prep. Time: 5 minutes · *Cooking Time: 4–5 minutes*

- 1 cup water
- 1 large head of cauliflower, cut into florets
- ½ cup butter
- 4 cloves garlic, crushed
- ½ tsp. salt
- ⅛ tsp. pepper

1. Pour the water into the inner pot of the Instant Pot, then place the steamer basket on top.
2. Put the cauliflower florets into the steamer basket.
3. Secure the lid and set the vent to sealing. Manually set the cook time for 1 minute on high pressure.
4. When cook time is up, manually release the pressure. Carefully remove the basket and discard the water from the inner pot. Wipe it dry.
5. Switch the Instant Pot to the Sauté function and let it get hot.
6. Add the butter to the inner pot and let melt. Once melted, add the garlic, cauliflower, salt, and pepper. Sauté for 2–3 minutes.

Serving suggestion:

This would go well served with Garlic and Lemon Chicken on page 87.

Lemony Garlic Asparagus

Hope Comerford, Clinton Township, MI

Makes 4 servings

Prep. Time: 5 minutes ♣ *Cooking Time: 1½–2 hours* ♣ *Ideal slow-cooker size: 2- or 3-qt.*

1 lb. asparagus, bottom inch (tough part) removed

1 Tbsp. olive oil

1½ Tbsp. lemon juice

3–4 cloves garlic, peeled and minced

¼ tsp. salt

⅛ tsp. pepper

1. Spray crock with nonstick spray.
2. Lay asparagus at bottom of crock and coat with the olive oil.
3. Pour the lemon juice over the top, then sprinkle with the garlic, salt, and pepper.
4. Cover and cook on Low for 1½–2 hours.

Air Fryer Adaptation:

1. Preheat the air fryer to 400°F for 5 minutes.
2. Toss the asparagus with the olive oil, lemon juice, garlic, salt, and pepper.
3. Arrange the asparagus into a single layer in the air fryer basket.
4. Cook at 400°F for 6–8 minutes, shaking the basket halfway through.

Serving suggestions:

- This would go well served alongside Honey Lemon Garlic Salmon on page 162.
- Garnish with diced pimento, garlic, and lemon zest.

Wild Mushrooms Italian

Connie Johnson, Loudon, NH

Makes 4–5 servings

Prep. Time: 20 minutes ❧ *Cooking Time: 6–8 hours* ❧ *Ideal slow-cooker size: 5-qt.*

- 2 large onions, chopped
- 3 large red bell peppers, chopped
- 3 large green bell peppers, chopped
- 2–3 Tbsp. olive oil
- 12-oz. pkg. oyster mushrooms, cleaned and chopped
- 4 cloves garlic, minced
- 3 fresh bay leaves
- 10 fresh basil leaves, chopped
- 1 tsp. salt
- 1½ tsp. pepper
- 28-oz. Italian plum tomatoes, crushed, or chopped

1. Sauté onions and peppers in oil in skillet until soft. Stir in mushrooms and garlic. Sauté just until mushrooms begin to turn brown. Pour into slow cooker.

2. Add remaining ingredients. Stir well.

3. Cover. Cook on Low 6–8 hours. Remove bay leaves and serve.

Serving suggestion:

These would go well served alongside Red Wine Apple Roast on page 125.

Desserts

Bananas Foster

Hope Comerford, Clinton Township, MI

Makes 6 servings

Prep. Time: 5–10 minutes · *Cooking Time: 1½–2 hours* · *Ideal slow-cooker size: 4-qt.*

1 Tbsp. olive oil
3 Tbsp. honey
3 Tbsp. fresh lemon juice
¼ tsp. cinnamon
Dash nutmeg
5 bananas (not green, but just yellow), sliced into ½-inch-thick slices

1. Combine the first five ingredients in the slow cooker.
2. Add the bananas and stir to coat them evenly.
3. Cover and cook on Low for 1½ to 2 hours.

Zucchini Chocolate Chip Bars

Hope Comerford, Clinton Township, MI

Makes 8–10 servings

Prep. Time: 10 minutes ❧ *Cooking Time: 2–3 hours*
Cooling Time: 30 minutes ❧ *Ideal slow-cooker size: 3-qt.*

- 3 eggs
- ¾ cup turbinado sugar
- 1 cup all-natural applesauce
- 3 tsp. vanilla extract
- 3 cups whole wheat flour
- 1 tsp. baking soda
- ½ tsp. baking powder
- 2 tsp. cinnamon
- ¼ tsp. salt
- 2 cups peeled and grated zucchini
- 1 cup dark chocolate chips

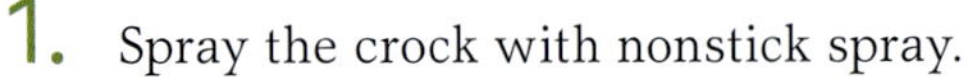

1. Spray the crock with nonstick spray.
2. Mix together the eggs, sugar, applesauce, and vanilla.
3. In a separate bowl, mix the flour, baking soda, baking powder, cinnamon, and salt. Add this to the wet mixture and stir just until everything is mixed well.
4. Stir in the zucchini and chocolate chips
5. Pour this mixture into the crock.
6. Cover and cook on Low for 2–3 hours. Let it cool in crock for about 30 minutes, then flip it over onto a serving platter or plate. It should come right out.
7. Slice into 8–10 pieces.

Carrot Cake

Colleen Heatwole, Burton, MI

Makes 10 servings
Prep. Time: 35 minutes *Cooking Time: 50 minutes*

⅓ cup canola oil
2 eggs
1 Tbsp. hot water
½ cup grated raw carrots
¾ cup flour and 2 Tbsp. flour, *divided*
¾ cup sugar
½ tsp. baking powder
⅛ tsp. salt
¼ tsp. ground allspice
½ tsp. ground cinnamon
⅛ tsp. ground cloves
½ cup chopped nuts
½ cup raisins or chopped dates
1 cup water

1. In a large bowl, beat the oil, eggs, and water for 1 minute.
2. Add the carrots. Mix well.
3. In another bowl, stir together the ¾ cup flour, sugar, baking powder, salt, allspice, cinnamon, and cloves. Add to the creamed mixture.
4. Toss the nuts and dates in a bowl with 2 Tbsp. of flour. Add to creamed mixture. Mix well.
5. Pour into greased and floured 7-inch springform pan and cover with foil.
6. Place the trivet into the Instant Pot and pour in the water. Place a foil sling on top of the trivet, then place the springform pan on top.
7. Secure the lid and make sure lid is set to sealing. Press Steam and set for 50 minutes.
8. When the cook time is over, release the pressure manually, then carefully remove the springform pan by using hot pads to lift the pan up by the foil sling. Place on a cooling rack until cool.

Lemon Pudding Cake

Jean Butzer, Batavia, NY

Makes 6 servings
Prep. Time: 15 minutes *Cooking Time: 50 minutes*

- 3 eggs, separated
- 1 tsp. grated lemon zest
- ¼ cup lemon juice
- 1 Tbsp. margarine or butter, melted
- 1½ cups half-and-half
- ½ cup sugar plus 2 Tbsp. sugar
- ¼ cup flour
- ⅛ tsp. salt
- 1 cup water

1. Beat the egg whites until stiff peaks form. Set aside.
2. Beat the egg yolks. Blend in the lemon zest, lemon juice, margarine, and half-and-half.
3. In separate bowl, combine the sugar, flour, and salt. Add to egg-lemon mixture, beating until smooth.
4. Fold into beaten egg whites.
5. Spoon into a greased and floured 7-inch springform pan. Cover with foil.
6. Place the trivet into the Instant Pot with the water. Place a foil sling on top of the trivet, then place the springform pan on top of the trivet.
7. Secure the lid and make sure lid is set to sealing. Press Manual and set time for 40 minutes.
8. Perform a quick release of the pressure when cooking time is done. Remove the springform pan carefully using hot pads with the foil sling and let cool on a cooling rack.

Upside-Down Apple Pie

Hope Comerford, Clinton Township, MI

Makes 6 servings

Prep. Time: 15 minutes · *Cooking Time: 6 hours* · *Ideal slow-cooker size: 6-qt.*

8 Gala apples, peeled, cored, and sliced
1½ tsp. apple pie spice
¾ cup milk
½ cup turbinado sugar
2 eggs
1½ cups Bisquick, *divided*
5 Tbsp. coconut oil, *divided*
1½ tsp. vanilla extract
¼ cup brown sugar

1. Line the crock with parchment paper and spray with nonstick spray.

2. Place the apples and apple pie spice into the crock and stir.

3. In a medium-sized bowl, mix the milk, turbinado sugar, eggs, ½ cup Bisquick, 2 Tbsp. melted coconut oil, and the vanilla. Pour this over the apples.

4. In a small bowl, mix the remaining Bisquick, coconut oil, and the brown sugar. It will be crumbly. Sprinkle this evenly over the contents of the crock.

5. Secure the lid of the slow cooker with some paper towels under it to absorb moisture.

6. Cook on Low for 6 hours.

Quick Yummy Peaches

Willard E. Roth, Elkhart, IN

Makes 6 servings

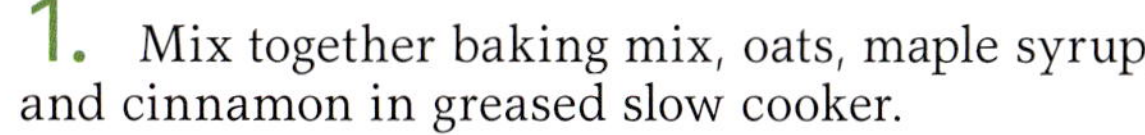

Prep. Time: 5–20 minutes ❧ *Cooking Time: 5 hours* ❧ *Ideal slow-cooker size: 3-qt.*

- ⅓ cup baking mix
- ⅔ cup oats
- ⅓ cup maple syrup
- 1 tsp. ground cinnamon
- 4 cups sliced fresh peaches
- ½ cup water

1. Mix together baking mix, oats, maple syrup, and cinnamon in greased slow cooker.
2. Stir in peaches and water.
3. Cook on Low for at least 5 hours. (If you like a drier cobbler, remove lid for last 15–30 minutes of cooking.)

Black and Blue Cobbler

Renee Shirk, Mount Joy, PA

Makes 12 servings

Prep. Time: 30 minutes ஃ *Cooking Time: 35 minutes* ஃ *Cooling Time: 30 minutes*

- 1 cup flour
- 1½ cups sugar, *divided*
- 1 tsp. baking powder
- ¼ tsp. salt
- ¼ tsp. ground cinnamon
- ¼ tsp. ground nutmeg
- 2 eggs, beaten
- 2 Tbsp. milk
- 2 Tbsp. vegetable oil
- 2 cups fresh blueberries
- 2 cups fresh blackberries
- ¾ cup water
- 1 tsp. grated orange peel
- 1 cup water
- Whipped topping or ice cream, *optional*

1. Combine flour, ¾ cup sugar, baking powder, salt, cinnamon, and nutmeg.
2. Combine eggs, milk, and oil. Stir into dry ingredients until moistened.
3. Spread the batter evenly over bottom of greased 1½-quart baking dish.
4. In saucepan, combine berries, ¾ cup water, orange peel, and the remaining ¾ cup sugar. Bring to boil. Remove from heat and pour over batter. Cover with foil.
5. Place the trivet into your Instant Pot and pour in 1 cup of water. Place a foil sling on top of the trivet, then place the baking dish on top.
6. Secure the lid and make sure lid is set to sealing. Press Manual and set for 35 minutes.
7. When cook time is up, allow the pressure to release naturally for 10 minutes, then release the remaining pressure manually. Carefully remove the baking dish by using hot pads to lift the foil sling. Place on a cooling rack, uncovered, for 30 minutes.
8. Once cooled, serve with a dollop of whipped topping or alongside a scoop of ice cream if you wish.

Blueberry Crinkle

Phyllis Good, Lancaster, PA

Makes 6–8 servings

Prep. Time: 15–20 minutes · *Cooking Time: 2–3 hours* · *Ideal slow-cooker size: 3- or 4-qt.*

⅓ cup turbinado sugar
¾ cup oats
½ cup flour
½ tsp. cinnamon
Dash kosher salt
6 Tbsp. coconut oil, cold
4 cups fresh blueberries
2 Tbsp. maple syrup
2 Tbsp. instant tapioca
2 Tbsp. lemon juice
½ tsp. lemon zest

1. Grease interior of slow-cooker crock.
2. In a large bowl, combine turbinado sugar, oats, gluten-free flour, cinnamon, and salt.
3. Using two knives, a pastry cutter, or your fingers, work coconut oil into dry ingredients until small crumbs form.
4. In a separate bowl, stir together blueberries, maple syrup, tapioca, lemon juice, and lemon zest.
5. Spoon blueberry mixture into slow-cooker crock.
6. Sprinkle crumbs over blueberries.
7. Cover. Cook 2–3 hours on Low, or until firm in the middle with juice bubbling up around the edges.
8. Remove lid with a giant swoop away from yourself so condensation on inside of lid doesn't drip on the crumbs.
9. Lift crock out of cooker. Let cool until either warm or room temperature before eating.

Nectarine Almond Crisp

Hope Comerford, Clinton Township, MI

Makes 8–9 servings

Prep. Time: 10 minutes ⁂ *Cooking Time: 2 hours* ⁂ *Ideal slow-cooker size: 3- or 4-qt.*

5 nectarines, cored and sliced
¼ cup slivered almonds
1 tsp. cinnamon
¼ tsp. nutmeg
¼ tsp. ginger
1 tsp. vanilla extract

Crumble:

1 cup gluten-free oats
½ cup almond flour
½ cup slivered almonds
1 tsp. cinnamon
¼ tsp. ginger
½ tsp. sea salt
2 Tbsp. honey
2 Tbsp. coconut oil, melted
2–3 Tbsp. unsweetened almond milk

1. Spray crock with nonstick spray.
2. In the crock, combine nectarines, almonds, cinnamon, nutmeg, ginger, and vanilla.
3. In a medium bowl, combine all the crumble ingredients. If the mixture is too dry, add a bit more honey or almond milk. Pour over the top of the nectarine mixture.
4. Cover and cook on Low for 2 hours.

Serving suggestion:

Serve over frozen vanilla Greek yogurt.

Strawberry Rhubarb Crisp

Hope Comerford, Clinton Township, MI

Makes 6–8 servings

Prep. Time: 30 minutes ⁂ *Cooking Time: 2–3 hours* ⁂ *Ideal slow-cooker size: 2½-qt.*

Filling:

1 lb. strawberries, quartered if medium or large

3 rhubarb stalks, halved and sliced

¼ cup turbinado sugar

2 Tbsp. flour

2 tsp. vanilla extract

Crisp:

¼ cup turbinado sugar

2 Tbsp. flour

½ tsp. cinnamon

Pinch salt

2 Tbsp. cold unsalted butter, sliced

½ cup old-fashioned oats

2 Tbsp. chopped pecans

2 Tbsp. chopped almonds

1. Spray your crock with nonstick spray.
2. Place the strawberries and rhubarb into the crock.
3. In a bowl, mix the sugar, flour, and vanilla. Pour this over the strawberries and rhubarb and stir to coat evenly.
4. In another bowl, start on the crisp. Mix the sugar, flour, cinnamon, and salt. Cut the butter in with a pastry cutter.
5. Stir in the oats, pecans, and almonds. Pour this mixture over the contents of the crock.
6. Cover and cook on Low for 2–3 hours.
7. The last half hour of cooking, remove the lid to help the crisp thicken.

Serving suggestion:

Serve over vanilla ice cream or on yogurt.

Metric Equivalent Measurements

If you're accustomed to using metric measurements, I don't want you to be inconvenienced by the imperial measurements I use in this book.

Use this handy chart, too, to figure out the size of the slow cooker you'll need for each recipe.

Weight (Dry Ingredients)

1 oz		30 g
4 oz	¼ lb	120 g
8 oz	½ lb	240 g
12 oz	¾ lb	360 g
16 oz	1 lb	480 g
32 oz	2 lb	960 g

Slow-Cooker Sizes

1-quart	0.96 l
2-quart	1.92 l
3-quart	2.88 l
4-quart	3.84 l
5-quart	4.80 l
6-quart	5.76 l
7-quart	6.72 l
8-quart	7.68 l

Volume (Liquid Ingredients)

½ tsp.		2 ml
1 tsp.		5 ml
1 Tbsp.	½ fl oz	15 ml
2 Tbsp.	1 fl oz	30 ml
¼ cup	2 fl oz	60 ml
⅓ cup	3 fl oz	80 ml
½ cup	4 fl oz	120 ml
⅔ cup	5 fl oz	160 ml
¾ cup	6 fl oz	180 ml
1 cup	8 fl oz	240 ml
1 pt	16 fl oz	480 ml
1 qt	32 fl oz	960 ml

Length

¼ in	6 mm
½ in	13 mm
¾ in	19 mm
1 in	25 mm
6 in	15 cm
12 in	30 cm

Recipe & Ingredient Index

A
air fryer
  Brussels Sprouts with Maple Glaze, 180
  Garden Chips, 190
  Honey Lemon Garlic Salmon, 162
  Lemony Garlic Asparagus, 195
  Potatoes with Parsley, 175
  Salmon with Chives, 163
  Thyme Roasted Sweet Potatoes, 172
allspice
  Carrot Cake, 203
almonds
  Nectarine Almond Crisp, 211
  Strawberry Rhubarb Crisp, 212
Apple Granola, 34
apple juice
  Braised Beef with Cranberries, 126
Apple Oatmeal, 32
apples
  Apple Oatmeal, 32
  Korean Beef, 129
  Red Wine Apple Roast, 125
  Spicy Roasted Butternut Squash, 179
  Upside-Down Apple Pie, 206
applesauce
  Giant Healthy Pancake, 17
  Zucchini Chocolate Chip Bars, 202
apricot preserves
  Garlic Mushroom Thighs, 88
asparagus
  Lemony Garlic Asparagus, 195
Aunt Twila's Beans, 174

B
bacon
  Brussels Sprouts with Maple Glaze, 180
  Fresh Zucchini with Bacon, 188
  Green Beans with Bacon, 187
Bacon, Spinach, and Parmesan Stuffed Meatloaf, 145
Bacon Ranch Red Potatoes, 177
Bananas Foster, 201
barley
  Beef Mushroom Barley Soup, 65
basil
  Bacon, Spinach, and Parmesan Stuffed Meatloaf, 145
  Batilgian, 152
  The Best Bean and Ham Soup, 59
  Butternut Squash Soup with Thai Gremolata, 81
  Cannellini Bean Soup, 72
  Cherry Tomato Pasta Sauce, 158
  Chicken and Vegetable Soup, 41
  Chicken Dinner in a Packet, 93
  Chicken Noodle Soup, 43
  Greek-Style Halibut Steaks, 164
  Herbed Fish Fillets, 166
  Insta Pasta à la Maria, 104
  Italian Chicken Wraps, 100
  Lasagna the Instant Pot Way, 141
  Pasta Primavera, 155
  Philly Cheese Steaks, 139
  Slow-Cooker Tomato Soup, 71
  Spinach and Mushroom Frittata, 25
  Spinach Frittata, 24
  Stuffed Cabbage, 140
  Turkey Sausage and Cabbage Soup, 52
  Twisted Shrimp Scampi à la Mamma Ree, 161
  Vegetables and Red Quinoa Casserole, 151
  Veggie Loaded Rice, 170
Basil Chicken, 89
Batilgian, 152
bay leaf
  Batilgian, 152
  The Best Bean and Ham Soup, 59
  Braised Beef with Cranberries, 126
  Carnitas, 113
  Chicken and Vegetable Soup with Rice, 42
  Four-Pepper Steak, 134
  Potato Leek Soup, 77
  Sweet Potato Soup with Kale, 76
  Wild Mushrooms Italian, 196
beans
  black
    Black Bean Soup with Fresh Salsa, 74
  cannellini
    Cannellini Bean Soup, 72
    Italian Shredded Pork Stew, 58
  garbanzo
    Basil Chicken, 89
    Chicken Casablanca, 96
  green
    Batilgian, 152
    Chicken and Vegetable Soup with Rice, 42
    Green Beans with Bacon, 187
    Minestrone, 73
    Sausage, Carrots, Potatoes, and Green Beans, 119
  pinto
    Aunt Twila's Beans, 174
    Minestrone, 73
beef
  chuck roast
    Carolina Pot Roast, 124
    Colorful Beef Stew, 66

Hungarian Beef with Paprika, 129
eye of round
Red Wine Apple Roast, 125
flank steak
Four-Pepper Steak, 134
ground
Bacon, Spinach, and Parmesan Stuffed Meatloaf, 145
Beef and Zucchini Casserole, 142
Lasagna the Instant Pot Way, 141
Stuffed Bell Peppers, 144
pot roast
Pot Roast, 123
round steak
Slow-Cooker Swiss Steak, 136
Swiss Steak with Carrots and Tomatoes, 137
skirt steak
Cuban Steak for Salad, 133
steak
Philly Cheese Steaks, 139
top round
Braised Beef with Cranberries, 126
Beef and Zucchini Casserole, 142
Beef Mushroom Barley Soup, 65
Beef with Broccoli, 132
beets
Slow-Cooker Beets, 182
Vegetables and Red Quinoa Casserole, 151
bell pepper
Broccoli and Bell Peppers, 191
Chicken Cheddar Broccoli Soup, 44
Chicken Chili Pepper Stew, 46
Colorful Beef Stew, 66
Egg Bites, 31
Fiesta Hashbrowns, 23
Four-Pepper Steak, 134
Hungarian Beef with Paprika, 129
Italian Chicken Wraps, 100
Philly Cheese Steaks, 139
Quinoa with Vegetables, 169
Rosemary Carrots, 185
Spanish Breakfast "Skillet," 29
Stuffed Bell Peppers, 144
Twisted Shrimp Scampi à la Mamma Ree, 161
Veggie Loaded Rice, 170
Wild Mushrooms Italian, 196
Zucchini Vegetable Pot, 105
The Best Bean and Ham Soup, 59
Best Smashed Potatoes, 178
biscuits
Biscuits and Gravy the Instant Pot Way, 19
Crustless Chicken Pot Pie, 103
Biscuits and Gravy the Instant Pot Way, 19
Black and Blue Cobbler, 209
Black Bean Soup with Fresh Salsa, 74
blackberries
Black and Blue Cobbler, 209
blueberries
Black and Blue Cobbler, 209
Blueberry Crinkle, 210
Braised Beef with Cranberries, 126
breadcrumbs
Turkey Meatball Soup, 51
breakfast
Apple Granola, 34
Apple Oatmeal, 32
Biscuits and Gravy the Instant Pot Way, 19
Breakfast Burrito Casserole, 20
Cinnamon Caramel Coffee Cake, 18
Delicious Shirred Eggs, 32
Easy Quiche, 28
Egg Bites, 31
Fiesta Hashbrowns, 23
Giant Healthy Pancake, 17
Italian Frittata, 26
Pumpkin Breakfast Custard, 36
Spanish Breakfast "Skillet," 29
Spinach and Mushroom Frittata, 25
Spinach Frittata, 24
Breakfast Burrito Casserole, 20
broccoli
Beef with Broccoli, 132
Chicken Cheddar Broccoli Soup, 44
Egg Bites, 31
slaw
Juicy Orange Chicken, 97
Broccoli and Bell Peppers, 191
broccolini
Pasta Primavera, 155
Brussels Sprouts with Maple Glaze, 180
Butternut Squash Soup with Thai Gremolata, 81

C

cabbage
Kielbasa and Cabbage, 117
Minestrone, 73
Stuffed Cabbage, 140
Turkey Sausage and Cabbage Soup, 52
Unstuffed Cabbage Soup, 50
cake
Carrot Cake, 203
Cinnamon Caramel Coffee Cake, 18
Lemon Pudding Cake, 204
Cannellini Bean Soup, 72
capers
Basil Chicken, 89
Batilgian, 152
caramel bits
Cinnamon Caramel Coffee Cake, 18
caraway
Hungarian Beef with Paprika, 129
Carnitas, 113
Carolina Pot Roast, 124
Carrot Cake, 203
carrots
Orange-Glazed Carrots, 186
Rosemary Carrots, 185
casserole
Beef and Zucchini Casserole, 142
Breakfast Burrito Casserole, 20
Vegetables and Red Quinoa Casserole, 151

cauliflower
Garlic Butter Cauliflower, 194
Potato Leek Soup, 77
Steamed Veggie Medley, 193
cayenne
Moroccan Spiced Stew, 67
celery seed
Chicken and Vegetable Soup with Rice, 42
cheese
Asiago
Minestrone, 73
Tuscan Chicken, 95
cheddar
Bacon Ranch Red Potatoes, 177
Chicken Cheddar Broccoli Soup, 44
Easy Quiche, 28
Egg Bites, 31
cottage
Lasagna the Instant Pot Way, 141
cream
Best Smashed Potatoes, 178
Creamy Potato Soup, 79
feta
Basil Chicken, 89
Greek-Style Halibut Steaks, 164
Gruyère
Spinach and Mushroom Frittata, 25
Mexican blend
Breakfast Burrito Casserole, 20
Monterey Jack
Fiesta Hashbrowns, 23
mozzarella
Fresh Veggie Lasagna, 157
Lasagna the Instant Pot Way, 141
Summer Squash Pie, 154
Swiss Steak with Carrots and Tomatoes, 137
Parmesan
Bacon, Spinach, and Parmesan Stuffed Meatloaf, 145
Beef and Zucchini Casserole, 142
Cannellini Bean Soup, 72
Delicious Shirred Eggs, 32
Fresh Veggie Lasagna, 157
Garden Chips, 190
Italian Chicken Wraps, 100
Italian Frittata, 26
Minestrone, 73
Mushroom Risotto, 149
Pasta Primavera, 155
Spinach Frittata, 24
Turkey Meatball Soup, 51
provolone
Philly Cheese Steaks, 139
Swiss Steak with Carrots and Tomatoes, 137
queso fresco
Spanish Breakfast "Skillet," 29
ricotta
Fresh Veggie Lasagna, 157
Cherry Tomato Pasta Sauce, 158
chicken
breast
Crustless Chicken Pot Pie, 103
Garlic and Lemon Chicken, 87
Italian Chicken Wraps, 100
Jazzed-Up Barbecue Pulled Chicken, 106
Juicy Orange Chicken, 97
Lime-Like Key West Chicken, 98
shredded
Insta Pasta à la Maria, 104
thigh
Basil Chicken, 89
Garlic and Lemon Chicken, 87
Garlic Mushroom Thighs, 88
Tuscan Chicken, 95
Chicken and Vegetable Soup, 41
Chicken and Vegetable Soup with Rice, 42
Chicken Casablanca, 96
Chicken Cheddar Broccoli Soup, 44
Chicken Chili Pepper Stew, 46
Chicken Dinner in a Packet, 93
Chicken Noodle Soup, 43
Chicken Rice Bake, 101
Chile-Lime Corn on the Cob, 183
chili powder
Black Bean Soup with Fresh Salsa, 74
Korean Beef, 129
Shredded Pork Tortilla Soup, 57
chipotle chiles
Spicy Roasted Butternut Squash, 179
chives
Salmon with Chives, 163
chocolate chips
dark
Zucchini Chocolate Chip Bars, 202
chorizo
Breakfast Burrito Casserole, 20
cider
Pork and Sweet Potatoes, 112
cilantro
Black Bean Soup with Fresh Salsa, 74
Butternut Squash Soup with Thai Gremolata, 81
Chicken Chili Pepper Stew, 46
Quinoa with Vegetables, 169
Cilantro Lime Rice, 171
cinnamon
Apple Granola, 34
Apple Oatmeal, 32
Bananas Foster, 201
Black and Blue Cobbler, 209
Blueberry Crinkle, 210
Carrot Cake, 203
Chicken Casablanca, 96
Cinnamon Caramel Coffee Cake, 18
Creamy Butternut Squash Soup, 80
Moroccan Spiced Stew, 67
Nectarine Almond Crisp, 211
Orange-Glazed Carrots, 186
Pumpkin Breakfast Custard, 36

Quick Yummy Peaches, 207
Spicy Roasted Butternut Squash, 179
Strawberry Rhubarb Crisp, 212
Zucchini Chocolate Chip Bars, 202
Cinnamon Caramel Coffee Cake, 18
cloves
Carrot Cake, 203
Pumpkin Breakfast Custard, 36
cobbler
Black and Blue Cobbler, 209
coconut milk
Butternut Squash Soup with Thai Gremolata, 81
coffee
Espresso Braised Beef, 128
Colorful Beef Stew, 66
coriander
Sweet Potato Soup with Kale, 76
corn
Chicken Chili Pepper Stew, 46
Chile-Lime Corn on the Cob, 183
Crustless Chicken Pot Pie, 103
cracker crumbs
Summer Squash Pie, 154
cranberries
Braised Beef with Cranberries, 126
cream
Tuscan Chicken, 95
Creamy Butternut Squash Soup, 80
Creamy Potato Soup, 79
Crustless Chicken Pot Pie, 103
Cuban Steak for Salad, 133
cumin
Aunt Twila's Beans, 174
Black Bean Soup with Fresh Salsa, 74
Carnitas, 113
Carolina Pot Roast, 124
Chicken Casablanca, 96
Chicken Chili Pepper Stew, 46
Cuban Steak for Salad, 133
Four-Pepper Steak, 134
Shredded Pork Tortilla Soup, 57
Spicy Roasted Butternut Squash, 179
custard
Pumpkin Breakfast Custard, 36

D
dates
Carrot Cake, 203
Delicious Shirred Eggs, 32
desserts
Bananas Foster, 201
Black and Blue Cobbler, 209
Blueberry Crinkle, 210
Carrot Cake, 203
Lemon Pudding Cake, 204
Nectarine Almond Crisp, 211
Quick Yummy Peaches, 207
Strawberry Rhubarb Crisp, 212
Upside-Down Apple Pie, 206
Zucchini Chocolate Chip Bars, 202
dill
Chicken Rice Bake, 101
Herbed Fish Fillets, 166
Quinoa with Spinach, 150

E
Easy Quiche, 28
Egg Bites, 31
eggplant
Batilgian, 152
eggs
Delicious Shirred Eggs, 32
Easy Quiche, 28
Italian Frittata, 26
Spinach and Mushroom Frittata, 25
Spinach Frittata, 24
escarole
Cannellini Bean Soup, 72
Turkey Meatball Soup, 51
Espresso Braised Beef, 128

F
Fiesta Hashbrowns, 23
fish
Greek-Style Halibut Steaks, 164
Herbed Fish Fillets, 166
Honey Lemon Garlic Salmon, 162
Salmon with Chives, 163
Fresh Veggie Lasagna, 157
Fresh Zucchini with Bacon, 188
frittata
Italian Frittata, 26
Spinach and Mushroom Frittata, 25
Spinach Frittata, 24

G
Garden Chips, 190
Garlic and Lemon Chicken, 87
Garlic Butter Cauliflower, 194
Garlic Mushroom Thighs, 88
Giant Healthy Pancake, 17
ginger
Chicken Casablanca, 96
Creamy Butternut Squash Soup, 80
Korean Beef, 129
Moroccan Spiced Stew, 67
Nectarine Almond Crisp, 211
Pumpkin Breakfast Custard, 36
granola
Apple Granola, 34
Greek-Style Halibut Steaks, 164
Green Beans with Bacon, 187
green chilies
Spanish Breakfast "Skillet," 29

H
halibut
Greek-Style Halibut Steaks, 164
ham
bone
The Best Bean and Ham Soup, 59
Easy Quiche, 28
Herbed Chicken, 92
Herbed Fish Fillets, 166
Honey Lemon Garlic Salmon, 162

hot sauce
- Chicken Cheddar Broccoli Soup, 44
- Egg Bites, 31
- Korean Beef, 129
- Stuffed Bell Peppers, 144

Hungarian Beef with Paprika, 129

I

instant pot
- Bacon Ranch Red Potatoes, 177
- Beef and Zucchini Casserole, 142
- Beef Mushroom Barley Soup, 65
- The Best Bean and Ham Soup, 59
- Biscuits and Gravy the Instant Pot Way, 19
- Black and Blue Cobbler, 209
- Black Bean Soup with Fresh Salsa, 74
- Braised Beef with Cranberries, 126
- Breakfast Burrito Casserole, 20
- Brussels Sprouts with Maple Glaze, 180
- Cannellini Bean Soup, 72
- Carnitas, 113
- Carrot Cake, 203
- Chicken and Vegetable Soup, 41
- Chicken Casablanca, 96
- Chicken Cheddar Broccoli Soup, 44
- Chicken Chili Pepper Stew, 46
- Chicken Dinner in a Packet, 93
- Chicken Noodle Soup, 43
- Chicken Rice Bake, 101
- Cilantro Lime Rice, 171
- Cinnamon Caramel Coffee Cake, 18
- Crustless Chicken Pot Pie, 103
- Delicious Shirred Eggs, 32
- Easy Quiche, 28
- Egg Bites, 31
- Fresh Zucchini with Bacon, 188
- Garlic Butter Cauliflower, 194
- Giant Healthy Pancake, 17
- Greek-Style Halibut Steaks, 164
- Green Beans with Bacon, 187
- Herbed Fish Fillets, 166
- Honey Lemon Garlic Salmon, 162
- Insta Pasta à la Maria, 104
- Korean Beef, 129
- Lasagna the Instant Pot Way, 141
- Lemon Pudding Cake, 204
- Lime-Like Key West Chicken, 98
- Mushroom Risotto, 149
- Pasta Primavera, 155
- Philly Cheese Steaks, 139
- Pork Chops with Potatoes and Green Beans, 114
- Potatoes with Parsley, 175
- Pot Roast, 123
- Quinoa with Spinach, 150
- Rosemary Carrots, 185
- Salmon with Chives, 163
- Sausage, Carrots, Potatoes, and Green Beans, 119
- Shredded Pork Tortilla Soup, 57
- Slow-Cooker Beets, 182
- Spinach and Mushroom Frittata, 25
- Split Pea Soup, 60
- Steamed Veggie Medley, 193
- Stuffed Cabbage, 140
- Summer Squash Pie, 154
- Sweet Potato Soup with Kale, 76
- Turkey Sausage and Cabbage Soup, 52
- Tuscan Chicken, 95
- Twisted Shrimp Scampi à la Mamma Ree, 161
- Unstuffed Cabbage Soup, 50
- Veggie Loaded Rice, 170

Insta Pasta à la Maria, 104
Italian Chicken Wraps, 100
Italian Frittata, 26
Italian seasoning
- Italian Shredded Pork Stew, 58
- Minestrone, 73
- Tuscan Chicken, 95

Italian Shredded Pork Stew, 58

J

jalapeño
- Chicken Chili Pepper Stew, 46
- Fiesta Hashbrowns, 23
- Four-Pepper Steak, 134

Jazzed-Up Barbecue Pulled Chicken, 106
Juicy Orange Chicken, 97

K

kale
- Italian Shredded Pork Stew, 58
- Sweet Potato Soup with Kale, 76

ketchup
- Korean Beef, 129
- Stuffed Bell Peppers, 144
- Tender and Tangy Ribs, 116

Kielbasa and Cabbage, 117
Korean Beef, 129

L

lamb
- Moroccan Spiced Stew, 67

lasagna
- Fresh Veggie Lasagna, 157

Lasagna the Instant Pot Way, 141
leek
- Potato Leek Soup, 77
- Split Pea Soup, 60

Lemon Pudding Cake, 204
Lemony Garlic Asparagus, 195
Lime-Like Key West Chicken, 98

M

maple syrup
- Blueberry Crinkle, 210
- Brussels Sprouts with Maple Glaze, 180
- Pumpkin Breakfast Custard, 36
- Quick Yummy Peaches, 207

marjoram
Colorful Beef Stew, 66
meatloaf
Bacon, Spinach, and Parmesan Stuffed Meatloaf, 145
Minestrone, 73
mint
Italian Frittata, 26
molasses
Pumpkin Breakfast Custard, 36
Moroccan Spiced Stew, 67
Mushroom Risotto, 149
mushrooms
baby bella
Mushroom Risotto, 149
Pasta Primavera, 155
Spinach and Mushroom Frittata, 25
Tuscan Chicken, 95
Beef and Zucchini Casserole, 142
Beef Mushroom Barley Soup, 65
Chicken and Vegetable Soup, 41
Chicken Dinner in a Packet, 93
Chicken Rice Bake, 101
Easy Quiche, 28
Fiesta Hashbrowns, 23
Fresh Veggie Lasagna, 157
Garlic Mushroom Thighs, 88
Insta Pasta à la Maria, 104
Lasagna the Instant Pot Way, 141
oyster
Wild Mushrooms Italian, 196
shiitake
Mushroom Risotto, 149
Steamed Veggie Medley, 193
Veggie Loaded Rice, 170
mustard
Brussels Sprouts with Maple Glaze, 180
dry
Jazzed-Up Barbecue Pulled Chicken, 106
Tender and Tangy Ribs, 116
Italian Chicken Wraps, 100

N
Nectarine Almond Crisp, 211
noodles
Chicken Noodle Soup, 43
Fresh Veggie Lasagna, 157
Lasagna the Instant Pot Way, 141
Turkey Soup, 49
nutmeg
Bananas Foster, 201
The Best Bean and Ham Soup, 59
Black and Blue Cobbler, 209
Creamy Butternut Squash Soup, 80
Nectarine Almond Crisp, 211
Orange-Glazed Carrots, 186

O
oatmeal
Apple Oatmeal, 32
oats
Apple Granola, 34
Blueberry Crinkle, 210
Nectarine Almond Crisp, 211
Quick Yummy Peaches, 207
Strawberry Rhubarb Crisp, 212
Orange-Glazed Carrots, 186
orange juice
Jazzed-Up Barbecue Pulled Chicken, 106
Juicy Orange Chicken, 97
Thyme and Garlic Turkey Breast, 90
oranges
Juicy Orange Chicken, 97
oregano
Bacon, Spinach, and Parmesan Stuffed Meatloaf, 145
Beef and Zucchini Casserole, 142
The Best Bean and Ham Soup, 59
Black Bean Soup with Fresh Salsa, 74
Carnitas, 113
Cherry Tomato Pasta Sauce, 158
Chicken Noodle Soup, 43
Fresh Veggie Lasagna, 157
Italian Chicken Wraps, 100
Italian Frittata, 26
Lasagna the Instant Pot Way, 141
Philly Cheese Steaks, 139
Stuffed Cabbage, 140
Summer Squash Pie, 154
Turkey Sausage and Cabbage Soup, 52
Turkey Soup, 49
Twisted Shrimp Scampi à la Mamma Ree, 161
Unstuffed Cabbage Soup, 50

P
pancakes
Giant Healthy Pancake, 17
paprika
Chicken and Vegetable Soup with Rice, 42
Colorful Beef Stew, 66
Herbed Chicken, 92
Philly Cheese Steaks, 139
smoked
Sausage, Carrots, Potatoes, and Green Beans, 119
sweet
Hungarian Beef with Paprika, 129
Sweet Potato Soup with Kale, 76
Tender and Tangy Ribs, 116
pasta
Fresh Veggie Lasagna, 157
Insta Pasta à la Maria, 104
Lasagna the Instant Pot Way, 141
Minestrone, 73
Pasta Primavera, 155
peaches
Quick Yummy Peaches, 207
peanuts
Butternut Squash Soup with Thai Gremolata, 81
peas
Chicken Noodle Soup, 43
Crustless Chicken Pot Pie, 103

Mushroom Risotto, 149
split
Split Pea Soup, 60
pecans
Cinnamon Caramel Coffee Cake, 18
Strawberry Rhubarb Crisp, 212
Philly Cheese Steaks, 139
poblano pepper
Breakfast Burrito Casserole, 20
pork
chops
Pork Chops with Potatoes and Green Beans, 114
chuck roast
Pork Roast and Vegetables, 111
loin
Shredded Pork Tortilla Soup, 57
shoulder
Carnitas, 113
Italian Shredded Pork Stew, 58
spareribs
Tender and Tangy Ribs, 116
Pork and Sweet Potatoes, 112
Pork Chops with Potatoes and Green Beans, 114
Pork Roast and Vegetables, 111
potatoes
Bacon Ranch Red Potatoes, 177
Best Smashed Potatoes, 178
Breakfast Burrito Casserole, 20
Creamy Potato Soup, 79
Crustless Chicken Pot Pie, 103
Fiesta Hashbrowns, 23
Kielbasa and Cabbage, 117
Pork Chops with Potatoes and Green Beans, 114
Pork Roast and Vegetables, 111
Potato Leek Soup, 77
Pot Roast, 123
Sausage, Carrots, Potatoes, and Green Beans, 119
Slow-Cooker Swiss Steak, 136
sweet
Carolina Pot Roast, 124
Creamy Butternut Squash Soup, 80
Italian Shredded Pork Stew, 58
Moroccan Spiced Stew, 67
Pork and Sweet Potatoes, 112
Sweet Potato Soup with Kale, 76
Thyme Roasted Sweet Potatoes, 172
Potatoes with Parsley, 175
potato flakes
The Best Bean and Ham Soup, 59
Potato Leek Soup, 77
pot pie
Crustless Chicken Pot Pie, 103
Pot Roast, 123
prosciutto
Italian Frittata, 26
Pumpkin Breakfast Custard, 36

Q
quiche
Easy Quiche, 28
Quick Yummy Peaches, 207
quinoa
Bacon, Spinach, and Parmesan Stuffed Meatloaf, 145
red
Vegetables and Red Quinoa Casserole, 151
Quinoa with Spinach, 150
Quinoa with Vegetables, 169

R
raisins
Carrot Cake, 203
ranch dressing mix
Bacon Ranch Red Potatoes, 177
Red Wine Apple Roast, 125
rhubarb
Strawberry Rhubarb Crisp, 212
ribs
Tender and Tangy Ribs, 116
rice
arborio
Mushroom Risotto, 149
brown
Beef and Zucchini Casserole, 142
Chicken Rice Bake, 101
Stuffed Cabbage, 140
Unstuffed Cabbage Soup, 50
Zucchini Vegetable Pot, 105
Chicken and Vegetable Soup with Rice, 42
Cilantro Lime Rice, 171
Stuffed Bell Peppers, 144
Veggie Loaded Rice, 170
risotto
Mushroom Risotto, 149
rolls
Philly Cheese Steaks, 139
rosemary
Cherry Tomato Pasta Sauce, 158
Espresso Braised Beef, 128
Herbed Chicken, 92
Pork Chops with Potatoes and Green Beans, 114
Sweet Potato Soup with Kale, 76
Rosemary Carrots, 185

S
sage
Herbed Chicken, 92
Italian Frittata, 26
Steamed Veggie Medley, 193
salmon
Honey Lemon Garlic Salmon, 162
Salmon with Chives, 163
salsa
Black Bean Soup with Fresh Salsa, 74
Breakfast Burrito Casserole, 20
sausage
breakfast
Biscuits and Gravy the Instant Pot Way, 19

chorizo
Breakfast Burrito Casserole, 20
Easy Quiche, 28
Kielbasa and Cabbage, 117
smoked
Sausage, Carrots, Potatoes, and Green Beans, 119
turkey
Fiesta Hashbrowns, 23
Spanish Breakfast "Skillet," 29
Turkey Sausage and Cabbage Soup, 52
Sausage, Carrots, Potatoes, and Green Beans, 119
sesame seeds
Broccoli and Bell Peppers, 191
Shredded Pork Tortilla Soup, 57
shrimp
Twisted Shrimp Scampi à la Mamma Ree, 161
slaw
broccoli
Juicy Orange Chicken, 97
slow cooker
Apple Granola, 34
Apple Oatmeal, 32
Aunt Twila's Beans, 174
Bacon, Spinach, and Parmesan Stuffed Meatloaf, 145
Bananas Foster, 201
Basil Chicken, 89
Batilgian, 152
Beef with Broccoli, 132
The Best Bean and Ham Soup, 59
Best Smashed Potatoes, 178
Black Bean Soup with Fresh Salsa, 74
Blueberry Crinkle, 210
Braised Beef with Cranberries, 126
Broccoli and Bell Peppers, 191
Butternut Squash Soup with Thai Gremolata, 81
Carnitas, 113
Carolina Pot Roast, 124
Cherry Tomato Pasta Sauce, 158
Chicken and Vegetable Soup, 41
Chicken and Vegetable Soup with Rice, 42
Chicken Chili Pepper Stew, 46
Chile-Lime Corn on the Cob, 183
Colorful Beef Stew, 66
Creamy Butternut Squash Soup, 80
Creamy Potato Soup, 79
Cuban Steak for Salad, 133
Espresso Braised Beef, 128
Fiesta Hashbrowns, 23
Four-Pepper Steak, 134
Fresh Veggie Lasagna, 157
Garden Chips, 190
Garlic and Lemon Chicken, 87
Garlic Mushroom Thighs, 88
Herbed Chicken, 92
Hungarian Beef with Paprika, 129
Italian Chicken Wraps, 100
Italian Frittata, 26
Italian Shredded Pork Stew, 58
Jazzed-Up Barbecue Pulled Chicken, 106
Juicy Orange Chicken, 97
Kielbasa and Cabbage, 117
Lemony Garlic Asparagus, 195
Minestrone, 73
Moroccan Spiced Stew, 67
Nectarine Almond Crisp, 211
Orange-Glazed Carrots, 186
Pork and Sweet Potatoes, 112
Pork Roast and Vegetables, 111
Potato Leek Soup, 77
Pot Roast, 123
Pumpkin Breakfast Custard, 36
Quick Yummy Peaches, 207
Quinoa with Vegetables, 169
Red Wine Apple Roast, 125
Shredded Pork Tortilla Soup, 57
Spanish Breakfast "Skillet," 29
Spicy Roasted Butternut Squash, 179
Spinach Frittata, 24
Strawberry Rhubarb Crisp, 212
Stuffed Bell Peppers, 144
Sweet Potato Soup with Kale, 76
Swiss Steak with Carrots and Tomatoes, 137
Tender and Tangy Ribs, 116
Thyme and Garlic Turkey Breast, 90
Thyme Roasted Sweet Potatoes, 172
Turkey Meatball Soup, 51
Turkey Sausage and Cabbage Soup, 52
Turkey Soup, 49
Vegetables and Red Quinoa Casserole, 151
Wild Mushrooms Italian, 196
Zucchini Chocolate Chip Bars, 202
Zucchini Vegetable Pot, 105
Slow-Cooker Beets, 182
Slow-Cooker Swiss Steak, 136
Slow-Cooker Tomato Soup, 71
soups
Beef Mushroom Barley Soup, 65
The Best Bean and Ham Soup, 59
Black Bean Soup with Fresh Salsa, 74
Butternut Squash Soup with Thai Gremolata, 81
Cannellini Bean Soup, 72
Chicken and Vegetable Soup, 41
Chicken and Vegetable Soup with Rice, 42
Chicken Cheddar Broccoli Soup, 44
Chicken Noodle Soup, 43
Creamy Butternut Squash Soup, 80
Creamy Potato Soup, 79

Minestrone, 73
Potato Leek Soup, 77
Shredded Pork Tortilla Soup, 57
Slow-Cooker Tomato Soup, 71
Split Pea Soup, 60
Sweet Potato Soup with Kale, 76
Turkey Meatball Soup, 51
Turkey Sausage and Cabbage Soup, 52
Turkey Soup, 49
Unstuffed Cabbage Soup, 50
sour cream
Summer Squash Pie, 154
soy sauce
Beef with Broccoli, 132
Broccoli and Bell Peppers, 191
Butternut Squash Soup with Thai Gremolata, 81
Korean Beef, 129
Spanish Breakfast "Skillet," 29
Spicy Roasted Butternut Squash, 179
spinach
Bacon, Spinach, and Parmesan Stuffed Meatloaf, 145
Egg Bites, 31
Fresh Veggie Lasagna, 157
Quinoa with Spinach, 150
Spinach and Mushroom Frittata, 25
Spinach Frittata, 24
Spinach and Mushroom Frittata, 25
Spinach Frittata, 24
Split Pea Soup, 60
squash
butternut
Butternut Squash Soup with Thai Gremolata, 81
Creamy Butternut Squash Soup, 80
Spicy Roasted Butternut Squash, 179
Vegetables and Red Quinoa Casserole, 151
summer
Summer Squash Pie, 154
yellow
Chicken and Vegetable Soup, 41
Steamed Veggie Medley, 193
stews
Chicken Chili Pepper Stew, 46
Colorful Beef Stew, 66
Italian Shredded Pork Stew, 58
Moroccan Spiced Stew, 67
Strawberry Rhubarb Crisp, 212
Stuffed Bell Peppers, 144
Stuffed Cabbage, 140
Summer Squash Pie, 154
sunflower seeds
Apple Granola, 34
Sweet Potato Soup with Kale, 76
Swiss Steak with Carrots and Tomatoes, 137

T

tamari
Lime-Like Key West Chicken, 98
tapioca
Blueberry Crinkle, 210
Fiesta Hashbrowns, 23
tarragon
Salmon with Chives, 163
Tender and Tangy Ribs, 116
thyme
Beef Mushroom Barley Soup, 65
Cherry Tomato Pasta Sauce, 158
Chicken Noodle Soup, 43
Espresso Braised Beef, 128
Garlic Mushroom Thighs, 88
Italian Chicken Wraps, 100
Philly Cheese Steaks, 139
Pork Chops with Potatoes and Green Beans, 114
Pork Roast and Vegetables, 111
Split Pea Soup, 60
Steamed Veggie Medley, 193
Thyme and Garlic Turkey Breast, 90
Turkey Soup, 49
Thyme and Garlic Turkey Breast, 90
Thyme Roasted Sweet Potatoes, 172
tomato
Batilgian, 152
Beef and Zucchini Casserole, 142
Cherry Tomato Pasta Sauce, 158
Chicken Casablanca, 96
Four-Pepper Steak, 134
Fresh Zucchini with Bacon, 188
Greek-Style Halibut Steaks, 164
Kielbasa and Cabbage, 117
Moroccan Spiced Stew, 67
Shredded Pork Tortilla Soup, 57
Slow-Cooker Swiss Steak, 136
Slow-Cooker Tomato Soup, 71
Spinach Frittata, 24
sun-dried
Tuscan Chicken, 95
Sweet Potato Soup with Kale, 76
Swiss Steak with Carrots and Tomatoes, 137
Turkey Sausage and Cabbage Soup, 52
Turkey Soup, 49
Wild Mushrooms Italian, 196
Zucchini Vegetable Pot, 105
tomato sauce
Fresh Veggie Lasagna, 157
Insta Pasta à la Maria, 104
Lasagna the Instant Pot Way, 141
Stuffed Cabbage, 140
tortillas
Breakfast Burrito Casserole, 20
Carnitas, 113
Italian Chicken Wraps, 100
turkey
breast
Thyme and Garlic Turkey Breast, 90

ground
Lasagna the Instant Pot Way, 141
Unstuffed Cabbage Soup, 50
Zucchini Vegetable Pot, 105
sausage
Fiesta Hashbrowns, 23
Turkey Sausage and Cabbage Soup, 52
Turkey Meatball Soup, 51
turkey sausage
Spanish Breakfast "Skillet," 29
Turkey Sausage and Cabbage Soup, 52
Turkey Soup, 49
turmeric
Moroccan Spiced Stew, 67
turnip
Braised Beef with Cranberries, 126
Espresso Braised Beef, 128
Tuscan Chicken, 95
Twisted Shrimp Scampi à la Mamma Ree, 161

U

Unstuffed Cabbage Soup, 50
Upside-Down Apple Pie, 206

V

Vegetables and Red Quinoa Casserole, 151
Veggie Loaded Rice, 170
vinegar
apple cider
Jazzed-Up Barbecue Pulled Chicken, 106
balsamic
Garlic Mushroom Thighs, 88
Slow-Cooker Beets, 182
Thyme and Garlic Turkey Breast, 90
rice
Korean Beef, 129
Tender and Tangy Ribs, 116
white wine
Italian Chicken Wraps, 100

W

walnuts
Apple Oatmeal, 32
wheat germ
Apple Granola, 34
Wild Mushrooms Italian, 196
wine
red
Red Wine Apple Roast, 125
white
Pork Roast and Vegetables, 111
Twisted Shrimp Scampi à la Mamma Ree, 161
Worcestershire sauce
Pork Roast and Vegetables, 111
Swiss Steak with Carrots and Tomatoes, 137
Tender and Tangy Ribs, 116
Zucchini Vegetable Pot, 105
wrap
Italian Chicken Wraps, 100

Y

yogurt
Greek
Best Smashed Potatoes, 178
Creamy Potato Soup, 79
Hungarian Beef with Paprika, 129

Z

zucchini
Chicken Casablanca, 96
Chicken Dinner in a Packet, 93
Fresh Veggie Lasagna, 157
Fresh Zucchini with Bacon, 188
Garden Chips, 190
Greek-Style Halibut Steaks, 164
Minestrone, 73
Pasta Primavera, 155
Zucchini Chocolate Chip Bars, 202
Zucchini Vegetable Pot, 105